Corfu Tales.

A 30 Year Love Affair

CW00400942

Preface.

In this book I will tell you about my visits to Corfu over the past thirty years, the holidays, buying a property in the village of Pelekas, the Corfu villages books and the Corfu charities. This is my story, I hope you enjoy it.

1. The Early Years.

2. Family Holidays.

3. Buying a Property.

4. Corfu villages eBook. Corfu Central.

5. Corfu North.

6. Corfu South.

7. Corfu Villages Printed Book.

1. The Early Years.

My story begins in the winter of 1986. I had been dating a girl for five years and we had come to the time when we would either get married and settle down or follow other dreams. My girlfriend at the time had been on a family holiday for a change the previous summer in Zakynthos and had fallen in love with Greece. When the winter came she asked me if I would mind if she could go to work in Corfu for the following summer as a tour representative for the Sunmed holiday company. I agreed but when the time came it broke our hearts and our relationship would never recover from the six month break. When she returned we tried to make a go of it but unfortunately we had both moved on and as she was due to go back to Corfu the following summer we decided to stay friends.

As the summer approached I met my now wife Ann and although we had been going out for a couple of weeks we had not made any plans for a summer holiday. At the same time I had an invite from my ex girlfriend to come to Corfu for a holiday. She was allowed one concessionary flight ticket as a tour representative and she wanted me to have it as she said Corfu was the kind of place I would fall in love with. I asked

Ann if she minded and being the kind person she is she said she didn't. I explained that she now had a boyfriend in Corfu and I would be going with my best friend Bob.

So in June of 1987 Bob and I headed off for a two week break near the resort of Dassia with our apartment being in the village of Kato Korakiana. I remember getting off the plane for the first time and feeling the heat and smelling the air as it hit me full on in my face. A short walk took us to the arrivals lounge where the security guard waved us through and simply glanced at our passports. We took a taxi to the apartment in Kato Korakiana and I gazed out of the window at the beauty of the view to the blue sea in the afternoon together with the green of the olive groves and the Cypress trees. This was the beginning of my love affair with Corfu.

We arrived late in the afternoon and were shown our apartment and as we caught up on all the latest gossip I decided to make a cup of tea for me and Bob. I boiled the kettle and went to pick it up but it was on a short cord and I spilt boiling water all over my leg and I was wearing shorts. I ran to the shower and turned the cold water tap on and sat there feeling sorry for myself. After five minutes I got up but then only just managed to reach the bed before I passed out!

Later that night we decided to eat at the nearby "Limeri taverna" down the road as we were a bit tired and I was still feeling a bit queasy. The taverna was covered in vines and the tables had checked tablecloths. There was a minor bird in the corner who was constantly talking. An old guitar hung on the wall with a collection of old photographs and paintings. The owner came out to greet us and gave us a menu in four languages. He was a big man with dark curly hair. I scanned the Greek part of the menu and proudly ordered Psito Kotopolo, Elliniki salada, Megali bira as I was practicing my Greek and I didn't think he could speak English. He stood there and a wry smile came over his face underneath the bushy Greek moustache. He looked around at the regular English, German and Dutch customers and replied, "Malista sir, Would you like that with chips or Greek potatoes". Well, we all burst out laughing and the taverna remains one of my favourite places to visit when we are around Dassia.

We had a nice meal, drank a few beers and a bottle of kokino krassi (red wine). As we paid the bill I stood up and felt very hot and ran to the gate where I bought back everything I had just digested. The owner was very upset as he thought he was responsible but Bob told him about the burnt leg and he felt better and proceeded to clean up the mess outside his taverna.

The next day we went to Dassia Beach and sunbathed with factor 2 coconut oil and a Greek guy from the Chandris hotel noticed that I had burnt my leg. He said the best thing for burns was to swim in the sea as the salt would help it dry out. So, we went swimming and we noticed a ski ramp in the distance. "Come on" Bob said, "I will race you there and then we can dive off the top of it". Bob dived off first and then beckoned me on. I said it looked a bit high but Bob said it was easy and stop being such a girl. I dived off but didn't get my hands forward enough to break the water and pulled a muscle in my neck. Two accidents in less than 24 hours!

Our first night out was on the Dassia strip in a bar called the Parallel Bar which was owned by Andreas from Pikoulatika and his Scottish wife. It was my ex's night off and she introduced us to all her rep friends. Everywhere we went we had discounted drinks, had great service and met the locals. We stopped out late, got drunk, walked back up the hill and woke up the next day with an almighty hangover after downing many a Metaxa and Coke.

The next day Bob asked around where we could hire a scooter. We were advised to get one from Alex and Christos who had a scooter rental shop in Gouvia. We met the family, got a good deal and had a couple of ouzos with the lads and their mother to seal the deal before heading back to Dassia. Bob was driving with me on the back and we had a short nap before planning our next night out.

That night we went with a couple of reps down to Ipsos to a bar called Michael's Cocktails. The owner was from Leicester and people were drinking cocktails called Ice tea, a lethal combination of white spirits, so we joined in. After dancing on the bar we all headed down the strip to Pirgi slapping tourists' backsides as we rode past them. As we came back the other way I reached over and slapped this guys backside but he turned around and my arm was thrown back. The scooter swerved and went in to a ditch of shale and we were heading for the wall. Bob somehow managed to drag us back on to the road and saved the day but after that we said do you think we ought to calm down a bit because at this rate we will be going home in a box.

On day three we were looking very dark as our factor 2 was working a treat. We went back down to Ipsos on the nighttime and we parked our chicken chaser outside the bar. We were talking to the owner behind the bar when we heard a banging noise outside but we took no notice at the time. I suggested that we go for a few drinks in Dassia, the others agreed, and we went outside to find our scooter in a ditch. We fetched it out but the handlebars were twisted and the speedometer was damaged which was not good. We went back in the bar to see if anybody had seen anything and luckily they had. A young English guy who worked for the Ipsos ski centre had had an arguement with someone, pulled out a baseball bat and decided to take it out on our scooter. We managed to get back to Kato, as we called it, riding with the handlebars at a 45 degree angle and put the front wheel between some railings to straighten the handlebars. In the morning my ex said we would have to tell the scooter shop lads because the damage would have to be paid for. She also said that the owner had been in the Greek Special Forces in the Army and was not a person to be messed with.

So, the next day we rode to Gouvia and showed him the damage. He said, "Do you know who did it"? we said "yes" and he said, "get in my car". He drove us in his Golf GTi at about 100 miles an hour down to Ipsos. We found the lad that had done the damage and the owner spoke to his boss who owned several business's in Ipsos and Dassia.

He told the lad to get in the car and said, "You owe me money for repairs and you have to pay me now". "You have two choices. I will take you to the bank and you will pay for the damage or you will have to pay the consequences. It's up to you"? (He actually mentioned his throat but I won't go there). We all went to the bank and he paid in full. Anyway, the next ten days were great as we visited lots of great beaches, villages and Corfu town. And yes, my ex was right, I did fall in love with Corfu and have loved the Island ever since.

When we got back to England I started seeing Ann on a regular basis and we fell in love...But that is another story...

It was June 1988 when we decided to head back to Corfu. I had been seeing Ann for a year now and this was to be our first holiday abroad together.

A few months before our local football team had just won the league and at the presentation night Ann had bought her best friend Tracey to the night and I introduced Bob to her. They got on great and started to go out together.

One night there was a few of us in the pub talking about holidays and we said we were going to Corfu. Bob and Tracey said they would like to come and so did a friend of ours called Dave.

Everything was sorted and we were all excited about our adventure until tragedy struck the day before we were due to fly out.

Ann and Tracey worked together for an insurance company and their manager had a heart attack the night before and had died.

Tracey was the senior clerk at the time and had worked with Tony for a few years so under the circumstances she said she would not be coming to Corfu. Bob said it would be difficult for him to come and leave Tracey in the situation she was in and we agreed that they should stay. I phoned Dave to give him the bad news and he asked if we were still going. We said we were, and he asked if we minded if he still came. We said not at all as there had been enough upset already.

It felt like home when we arrived back in Kato and I couldn't wait to show Ann and Dave all the great places we had been the year before. We dumped our suitcases, had a shower and walked down the road to the Red Penguin bar where we used to have last drink the year before. Spiros the owner was pleased to see us and we had a few drinks. Next door was a Travel Agency owned by a Swiss lady called Dora. She had sorted out the apartment for us and arranged a lift to Gouvia to hire a couple of scooters.

The owners of the scooter hire shop and their mother greeted us as if we were long lost family. The ouzo came out and after a few glasses the bikes were ready.

We went down to Michael's cocktails in Ipsos and then to the Parallel bar in Dassia. I introduced Ann and Dave to all the people we had met the year before and we had a great night. When we left the bar we got on our scooters and as there was some gravel between the bar and the road I said to Dave to be careful. I pushed my scooter over the gravel but the front wheel gave way and with Ann on the back I lost my balance and over we went. No problem I thought as I picked the bike up, I started the scooter and got ready to go.

No! No! Steve, said Andreas the owner. You are not riding the scooter home, I forbid it, you will kill yourself. I said I was ok and that I slipped on the gravel but he wouldn't have it so we had to leave it there and walk two kilometres back and uphill to Kato village. Dave decided to leave his as well and we just laughed all the way back.

The next day it was lunchtime by the time we got Dave out of bed. We walked back to the bar and picked up the scooters. We headed back to Dassia but it was looking a bit overcast. I said we might as well have a drive up the east coast if we can't sunbathe but it had started to rain as we got to Ipsos.

We parked up and went into a taverna for something to eat. The clouds were still gathering so we had a couple of beers and talked about the strange turn of events that had led us to here. Then it rained and we ordered more beers, ouzo and Metaxa. Ann was ok until Dave and I decided to take our beers and the lilo into the sea in the pouring rain.

We headed back for a nap and later went down through Ipsos and Pirgi to the village of Agios Markos. Spiros from the Red Penguin lived there and said we ought to go to the Moonshine Bar. They brewed their own Krasi, red and rose wine.

We poured ourselves a copper tankard each and settled down by the open view across the bay when bang. A crack of lightening came like a thunderbolt from Zeus. The noise was deafening and it felt as if was right above us. This carried on for half an hour. The locals just laughed at us as we were the only tourists in there. It was a fantastic display of electric current running through the moonlit sky and an array of the colours of blue, pink and grey I will never forget.

We eventually got up to pay and the owner asked how many tankards we had drunk. I said I had know idea, I thought you were keeping count?

Ann had forgiven us by now and said that Dave and I had drunk three and she had drunk two. The owner said pay me for three? "What" I said. "I will buy you a round and your Greek friends have bought the men a round. So you owe me for three" What a gesture and what nice people. "I told you the Greeks were great didn't I" when we got back.

 Before Ann and I went to bed that night I said we ought to go to Paleokastritsa and see the view from Bella Vista tomorrow, the only problem we had was getting Dave out of bed before 1.00pm.

 When he was asleep I took his watch off his wrist and turned it forward two hours. I got up at 9.00 am and told Dave it was 11.00 am. We arrived in Paleo for breakfast at 10.00/12.00 and Dave looked at the lunch menu and complained of being tired. I said I'm not surprised mate, it's 10.00 am in the morning and you've only had three hours sleep!

We had a great first week and on the second week we went to a village festival (Panigiri) at Doukades. My Greek was just good enough to read the sign on the Paleo road the week before.

We went cross country bypassing Ano Korakiana and Skripero and followed the crowd to a large field. There was a Greek band playing, tins of beer in big tubs of cold water and Lamb on the spit.

We got drinks and sat down on one of the long plastic tables. I felt confident enough to order the meat in Greek so I joined the queue for the food. But people were shouting over me and pushing in the queue.

Suddenly, I was lifted off the floor and a shout from behind me ordered the food.

I looked round and standing there was this huge guy about six foot six and built like a brick out house!

I am Spiros the seaman from Zigos he said, sit down and have your food I will come and talk to you later.

There must have been five hundred people there that night. Spiros came over and we had a great chat, he invited us to his house in Zigos the next day and introduced us to the only other English family there.

We sat down and had a few beers with them, they were a nice family. We found out later that he was the director of the original series of "My Family and other Animals"! We met some lovely people and we had a great holiday.

Ann and I decided to get married in 1989 and after a meeting with the vicar from our local church we set a date. The only problem was it would be in eighteen months time. We didn't want to wait that long so looked into getting married at Gretna Green in Scotland.

On November 13th, just six weeks later we had a civil marriage on the green and then a mock wedding at the old Blacksmiths over the Anvil. Bagpipes were played and the tourists took our photos. When we got back home we had a big party for friends and family It was a great experience and we have never looked back since.

Our honeymoon was to be a two week holiday in Paxos at the end of April which was the first weeks of the season.

We flew to Corfu and took the three hour boat down to Lakka arriving at about 9.00pm in the evening. It was getting dark, it had been a choppy sea and our flight had been delayed but, at last we had arrived.

As we took our luggage off the boat the villagers came to the harbour to meet us and help us carry them into the rooms. We were the first tourists of the season and there were thirty of us only for the first week.

We were all starving and hadn't eaten for hours so we decided to have a quick wash and brush up and all meet in the only taverna that was open on the harbour front.

I had been on a one year Greek Language course to learn the basics and how to order food so I was looking forward to it.

But everything that we asked for they didn't have? "Is my Greek that bad?" "No, said the lady, my brother has gone to the local butchers house to get him out of bed. He will have a look in his shop to see if he has got what you want" I had Gavros (small fish) for a starter as I had never tasted it before. A huge plate came but, after a couple of mouthfuls I thought, I don't like this.

We were sitting by the open window and there was a skinny black and white cat sitting there. I put a couple of fish on the ledge and it was mayhem.

Cats of all colours, shapes and sizes came piling through the window for their supper. The taverna was in chaos as it filled with the local Top Cat gang !

"We don't feed the cat's inside the taverna" the lady said in a quiet and friendly voice.

Lakka was quite underdeveloped in those days and it didn't take long to get to know the bar and taverna owners.

One night we went to the Mister Mouse taverna in the old square. It was a rustic place with an old kitchen. The chef had a cigarette in his mouth as he cooked but he had said he would get me a lobster if I wanted so I had ordered it the day before.

It came whole on a big plate with a hammer and a bowl of garlic, lemon and oil dip.

I had no idea what to do with it so Mr. Mouse opened it up and I ate the meat in the body. When I had finished he said I hadn't eaten the claws, put one in his mouth and crunched it open with his teeth then handed it back to me. I broke one open, ate it and said that I had had enough, he said "I will never cook you lobster again".

We went up to the Serano bar for couple of beers and met a guy who had a forty foot yacht. He said he was going to start a business taking tourists around Paxos and would a few of us like to go on his trial run tomorrow, free of charge.

The next day we joined his boat and it wasn't long before he asked me to help with the sails and before I knew it I was second mate and sailing the boat around the Island.

It was a beautiful trip as it was getting dark as we headed back to Lakka. The wind had got up and after a very hot April day it had now become cold.

We got back to the room, had a shower and headed for the Serano bar. When I walked in I felt hot, a bit sick and faint. I could see myself in the mirror and I was bright red. I had major sunstroke and just lay on the bench like a wet lettuce.

The next day I was back to normal and even managed to water ski as one of the bar owners had a speedboat and a wetsuit and had asked me if I would like to ski and again this was all free.

That night in the bar I asked why there was a very large Metaxa bottle with a tap on it at the bar. The owner said it was a special bottle and you can drink as much as you like but you have to pass a test.

"Ok, I said what do I have to do?" He said, "you put your head under the tap, pour a mouthful and then run around the block, sit down and get ready for the next one".

I asked him what the record was and he said four laps. "You won't do it, believe me". I managed seven laps and broke the record. I was young and daring in those days.

The next day we were going to Anti Paxos for the day. We were going on a small fishing boat and I sat at the back by the engine. The smell of the diesel made me feel a bit sick. The captain gave us an apple and then an ouzo for the journey. After the Metaxa the night before my body couldn't take anymore. I rushed down into the cabin, grabbed a bucket and was violently sick.

Then the bad news, the bucket had a huge hole in the bottom so my feet were covered in apple sauce.

We had a great honeymoon and met some great people. Ann and I did have some very romantic times there and enjoyed sunbathing in the day and eating out on the nights.

A few months later a man came in the shop where I was working and said he was a ventriloquist on a cruise ship and he had been to Lakka, a beautiful place on Paxos near Corfu. I said I had been on honeymoon there in April. He said "There is a famous story of a crazy Englishman who drank Metaxa from the bottle and held the record for the most laps around the village. They say it will never be beaten?

Most people only managed one or two laps of the block".

Ha ha, I said, "That was me!"

2. Family holidays.

When our first child was born we couldn't afford a holiday abroad. Eva May came into our lives and changed our lives completely. We named her after a female customer of mine at the time who was from a Greek Cypriot family who had a fish and chip shop a couple of miles away from our house. She was a lovely lady with a petite figure, long black hair, blue eyes, a Greek nose and olive skin. She used to come into the shop and buy clothes for two of her boys. I had just quitted my job as a manager of a men's fashion shop and had decided to open my own shop. We had recently moved to a bigger house so life was a bit of a gamble at the time. We had spent a few holidays in Wales and begged and borrowed caravans from friends and family but we missed Corfu and the Greek way of life.

We really needed to replace the windows all over the house as the wooden frames were ageing as the house was built in 1928. But if we were to replace a couple of windows a year instead of buying them all in one go then maybe we could stretch to a holiday abroad? When Eva was a one year old we decided to bite the bullet and take a one week holiday to Corfu and to the resort of Agios Gordios. Ann and I had stayed there a few years previous and we liked the fact that it had many tavernas and a fantastic sandy beach. We stayed at Katerina's, next door to the Robin's nest bar and it had a nice swimming pool with a small shallow section for children. We knew quite a few of the taverna owners from previous visits and they made a big fuss of Eva with her black hair and bright eyes. They would bring us or borrow a baby chair with two hooks either side that fitted onto the table. She would be paraded around the tables and taken into the kitchen to meet the Mitera (Mother) who would be cooking our evening meals. It's a great resort and I would have no hesitation in recommending families and couples to stay there for a holiday. We had a great holiday that year and we still pop down to Agios Gordios occasionally to see old friends and of course they can't believe how much the children have grown.

The following year we decided to go back to Parga on the mainland. This holiday would be with my Mother and

Father. We had been there a few years before and stayed at the Rezi hotel but now they had a swimming pool which was a bonus. Parga is a town 50 kilometres south of Igoumenitsa port and easily reached from Corfu. It has a town beach (Krioneri) a harbour and a Kastro (Castle) at the hilltop with a walk downhill to a huge crescent sandy beach on the other side. The town houses tumble down from the Kastro to the sea and is it is very picturesque. There are over one hundred tavernas and restaurants and many Europeans return year after year. The reason we like it is that you can reach Paxos and Corfu if you fancy a mini holiday. This was the year that the smoking ban came into force on aeroplanes. Dad was a heavy smoker and we hadn't told him there was a ban. He wasn't very happy but was placated when he realised he could smoke in the airport. We had a great time but after this Dad never flew abroad again. Instead he and Mom would travel to Europe by coach.

When baby number two came along two years later we contemplated taking Eva and the baby for a one week holiday abroad. Robert David (Bobby) was named after the great Manchester United and England footballer. Not that I am a Manchester United fan but I remember going outside for a cigarette when he was born and trying to think of a name for him when I thought about the great footballers of the winning England football team. Bobby Moore, Bobby Charlton. Yes, we would call him Bobby. It was a good job I didn't name him after one of the great Brazilian players as I think Edson Arantes do Nascimento (Pele) would not have gone down too well with my wife Ann.

When Eva was eighteen months old we went to Lanzarote for a winter break in February. This was our first all inclusive holiday and we could only afford one week as it was quite expensive in those days. It was a novelty to be able to eat and drink when the mood took us and the soft drinks, ice cream and children's club was available for Eva. Lanzarote was ok, with it's man made beach, the hot geysers in the mountains and white buildings. But, where were the green olive trees? Where were the tavernas, where were the locals and the culture?

With Eva now aged three and Bobby aged one we decided to try another seven day Thomson all inclusive holiday to the resort of Porto San Miguel in Ibiza. We thought that would suit the children as everything was on site. There was the usual food all day, drinks, a choice of using the facilities and restaurants of the three hotels in the small bay. There was a lovely sandy beach, kids club, games for children and adults and nightly entertainment. The children were a bit young and clingy to use the kids clubs and although the people we met were very nice they were all English and quite tribal. When we sat down for breakfast there would be a family on the next table sporting their football shirts. Where were the mix of Europeans we were used to meeting on holiday? Well, that was it for me and when Eva said that she didn't want to use the kids club and she would rather go to the beach with us it was time to head back to Greece.

For the following two years we went back to Parga and did a two centre holiday with Paxos. The greenery, locals and culture had returned but it was not Corfu.

As you can probably gather, we were a little mixed up by this time. We loved our time in Parga and Paxos and as you know when you meet the locals it is hard not to return as the generosity of the Greek people is so infectious. Well the next holiday would be the Ford family on tour. We would fly to Corfu and have a four days in Agios Gordios, four days in Dassia, on to Paxos for three days, a couple of nights in Parga and a night in Corfu town at the Atlantis hotel.

We would also take my mother and my sister Judi this time. In Agios Gordios we stayed at Katerina's again as the Sea Breeze was always booked well in advance. We ate at the Sea Breeze on their Greek night and had Kontosouvli, chunks of pork from the spit, one of my favourite Greek dishes. We danced all night and it reminded me of the first time Ann and I had stayed at the Sea Breeze. Breakfast or brunch would be on the beach or from the Souvlaki shop. We would all huddle round the table at the apartment overlooking the swimming pool and gorge on Giros pitta with Greek salad. I would play a few songs on the guitar I had bought out with me and the kids would jump about on the bed and sing their own lyrics. The other nights we ate out at Alex in the Garden, Sebastian's and The Mermaid. All good tavernas and always good service. The next stop was a half an hour taxi to our old haunt, Dassia and the lovely Artemis apartments owned by of Karen Trifona and her husband. The first place we would visit was the taverna Limeri up the hill in the close village of Kato Korakiana. This as you now know was the first place I had ever eaten many years before. Well, yes of course he remembered me as all good Greek owners do. The minor bird was still there and the old guitar was still hanging on the wall inside. The place looked the same but the staff had changed and so had the village a little. Opposite the Limeri was now a Greek bar and another taverna up the hill. But the Limeri had many returning visitors and is still going strong even though a friend of mine who lives in Kinopiastes told me that the owner had died...He was her cousin.

We ate our meal and walked downhill to the Red Penguin bar to see our old friend Spiros and his wife Dina. Spiros is an absolute superstar.

We used to go down to Ipsos for late night drinks when we first came to Corfu we would stop there for a last drink on our way home. He would be waiting to close the bar as the last people left and we would arrive on the scooters and pap the horn as we approached. Yasou Spiro file mou! I would shout. Teleftaio! One last one for the road! Oxi he would say. But he always gave in and we made it worth his while with an order of megalo bira (Big beer) or Metaxa pendi asteria kai Coke (Metaxa five star and Coke). And a couple of special pizzas to make sure the till was a bit fuller before we headed home. His English has always been good as he used to have the welcome meetings for the tour companies when their guests arrived. Sun Med, Libra holidays, Grecian, do you remember those? All gone now...

Anyway, Spiros was pleased to see us and we talked about the old days and he said how Eva had grown and made Bobby laugh. We took some old photographs to show him, yes remember photographs? After a few beers he drove us back up the Dassia strip as we were staying at the start of the resort and he was at the end of the resort where the turning is to Kato Korakiana and the short walk to Ipsos. Many of the people we had met in Dassia had either closed down or moved on over the years so we ate out at different places and enjoyed our stay.

The most memorable day for me was the day we spent on a hidden beach near to the Artemis where we were staying. Karen told us to walk down the dirt track opposite and we would have a small beach to ourselves. We walked down the track of lined with Eucalypsos trees for about ten minutes and to our surprise there it was. A small beach with a thirty foot tree in the middle which was perfect for a shaded afternoon. The sea was a bit rocky here so you had to be careful when entering the water. We wandered with the kids to the left and found a sea cucumber. I showed Bobby how to squeeze it so the water spurted out but told him we must put him back now as he would die if we continued. A walk to the right of the beach and a trek through the undergrowth exposed a delapidated church. This was an adventure! We sat down together to have a bite to eat from our packed lunch and I realised one of my greatest dreams. When my brother in law had enticed me into learning to play the guitar the year before I had agreed and said that if I did I would play for my wife and kids on a beach on Corfu. So, for a year I had practiced, learned a few songs and finally achieved it. Years later I became a singer and rhythm guitar player in a Mod band but that's a different story.

Next stop was the beautiful Island of Paxos. We caught the number seven bus from Dassia and walked to the new port to catch the Dolphin down to Paxos. After one hour we arrived in Gaios and waited for the bus to take us North to Lakka where Ann and I had spent our honeymoon. A bit different to the three hour ferry we had taken when we went for the first time. The bus was full of children as they had just come out of school, they were boisterous but they made sure that we all had a seat. Endearing and good manners too. We were staying above the Serano bar in the owners accommodation. It's not what you know! Thanks to Sharon and Touli and

God bless you Touli as you go to sleep with the Gods. If you know Lakka, it is a very small bay on the northeast tip of Paxos. The beaches are nothing to write home about but the harbour is delightful and the small village which doubles as the resort is a great and safe place for children. We talked to the different owners of the tavernas and we agreed that Paxos was more expensive these days but the quality of the food accommodation had gone up to a higher level. A nice few days were spent and we said our goodbye's as we headed to Parga on the mainland.

The next day we begged a lift on the day trip boat from Paxos to Parga. The captain agreed a price for the one way ticket and we were there. We stayed at the pension Vergis because we knew the family from when we first came to Parga years ago. The rooms were a short walk from Piso Krioneri beach and the first night we took our visitors (mom and Judi) to our favourite taverna there. The Golfo is situated at the start of the town and has access the small beach. It is a mixture of small stones and shingle giving way to sand as you enter the sea. There are rocks either side and it is sheltered from the wind. I hadn't noticed that the side entrance with a wooden boarded path had been built since our last visit and proceeded to walk through the open door at the front of the building as we had always done. We walked down the corridor and down the steep stairs to the restaurant. Christos was waiting for us at the bottom. Welcome my friends he said. I asked him how he knew we were coming. He said only the very first customers and friends use front door to my house to enter the taverna and he would always be there to greet them no matter how busy he was.

A catch up with Leandros and Michalis at the Captains bar and Pavlos at the new bar on the strip. Pavlos was keen to show us his new bar as it was very trendy then and the start of a new era for Greece and the Islands. Bar lights, comfy chairs, low and high. Lighted walls with local small brick walls. Antique pots in dotted recess's. All very nice. We sat down and talked and I broke away for a few minutes to walk the children up the harbour in their pushchairs to get them to sleep and returned for a well earned beer. Pavos said, Steve, you have to see the toilets, they are fantastic. I thought at last they have got the message. Toilets are very important to tourists why has it taken so long for you to get the message! So, we walk through a corridor and it is beautifully lit with mirrors, tiles and basins made in Italy. And then he shows me the men's toilet. Tiled and lit he was very proud and then I looked down. There it was, a small hole in the ground like an old French toilet. I smiled and left with a tinge of disappointment. But the worse was to come. Ten minutes later and I had a Greek tummy. I needed to go to the new toilet and now! I released my belt and jeans and aimed fearing the worst. Bingo! It was a bulls eye. Wow! It actually works. But what was in the ladies?

When we first came to Parga we met the captain of the Apollon Parga football team. They were a good side and were semi professional. They used to play the teams in Corfu and beat most of them apart from the Corfu town team who were and still are in and out of the Super league and second division. My mate Bob and I were kicking a ball around on the Parga pitch one day where we were playing hit the bar from outside of the area. Parga had a match in an hour or so and they let the younger players come out to practice. We knew we had to leave now but they wouldn't let us. They wanted to know who we played for in England and arranged a game for us to play. Well, me and Bob just played our own game and they loved it. The Parga team came on to play and another Christos the captain thanked us for keeping the young players and the supporters (1,000) happy for the build up to the match and handed me a track suit top. It was his top and coloured in red, white and blue with Apollon Parga on the back. I have still got the track top to this day. I have been to Parga recently and Christos the footballer who has a giros shop now still remembers our great times from many years ago and we are still good friends.

It was time to head back to Corfu. We took a taxi with an old bar fly we knew and he showed us a few ruins and archaeological sites on the way back to the ferry port of Igoumenitsa. The trip from the mainland to Corfu is a wonder. As you approach the emerald

Island the sun hits the water like a million stars. The light blue of the sky contrasting with the dark blue of the Ionian sea is a picture to behold. The sight of Corfu town and the Venetian buildings are the first sights you will see with the Old Fortress and the new port. Followed gently by the New Fort and the Old port. A bit confusing I know but you will get used to it as you visit more often.

We booked into the Atlantis hotel and I asked in Greek if we could have a room with a sea view. Georgios said yes and I was happy. Then, A voice behind me said, Hi Steve, How are you! It was Richard, a customer of mine from many years ago from Coventry who had given up a highly paid job to become a missionary in Albania. As you may know, Albania is a very poor country and Richard and his team were supplying medical supplies, supporting the poorest families and preaching the word of Christianity. We dropped the suitcases off, had a shower and re-joined him as he said he would take us to an Albanian taverna which was owned by a family he knew. We strolled up from the new port, through the winding narrow streets of the old quarter and arrived at the taverna at around 9.00 pm. We were hungry but there was not a lot of food left as this taverna is mainly a daytime or early evening place where the meals are cooked freshly in the morning and placed in stainless steel trays so you can order a variety of plates for the table to share. I didn't realised at the time but they also sold giros and meat from the grill. It was probably the worst meal we have ever had on Corfu. The chicken from the oven was the size of a sparrow with hardly any meat on the bone. The green beans were drenched in olive oil but the chips were hand cut and nicely fried. After the meal we said our goodbyes and agreed to keep in touch through the monthly newsletter that they sent out from the Albanian headquarters. I liked what he was doing for the poor people and I did arrange a few clothing donations to them over the next few years but the logistics were difficult. Unless you can take the clothing to Corfu yourself and arrange for someone to take it over to Albania then the costs involved with transportation from the UK are too high.

When we left the taverna we headed for a nightcap on the Liston. The Liston was build in 1807 by the French in the style of the Rue de Rivoli in Paris. We headed for the oldest café towards the top end of the building called Zisimos. This was the oldest café on the Liston and had the history. I ordered an Ouzo with water and thankfully it came with a good size meze! Eva asked me the name of the taverna we had eaten at and I said that I hadn't noticed the sign above the door. Then we will call it "Greases" she said. I have returned to the taverna over the past few years and I have to say it is excellent. The food is superb and I often have lunch there at Nino's.

We had a great two week holiday but where would we go next year? We liked all the places we had visited in Greece, especially the Ionian area. The next few years we would return to Corfu and make a decision that would change our lives forever.

In some ways I am so pleased that the Greek taverna and restaurant has evolved and become more European and more to my taste. But in other ways I miss the old Greek tavernas. Whilst the new ones retain the Greek menu and have improved facilities (the toilets were awful) back then. Many are now up to date and indeed state of the art. With mass tourism now a distant memory they have stepped up to the plate and transformed their eateries into top class places we are proud to show our friends and family. The younger generation must have fought long and hard with the parents to get them to agree to the investment not to mention the transformation. The discerning new customer has quite rightly demanded change and the Corfiot's have mostly delivered.

So, what am I complaining about? When I first came to Corfu and ate out in the evening I as horrified at the choice on the menu. A choice of a few Greek main meals with green beans and potatoes served in olive oil? Kleftiko, stifado, sofrito? I soon learned the words for, Do you have? Mi pos exete? What is this? Ti einai afto? In most places the tables and chairs were old, the décor was old fashioned and the owners were as old as my grandparents. But...the hospitality was unique. The reception on entering a new place would be as if you were a long lost son and daughter. The food was cooked in the daytime by Mitera, the Mother and Ya Ya, the grandmother. The vegetables and salad was fresh from the owners fields. The meat was a bit tough if you had a steak but was beautiful from the oven. The fish was caught from the Ionian sea and delivered the same day...The entertainment was improvised and done on the spur of the moment depending who was around and who was prepared to get involved. I never thought I would miss the old days on Corfu, and in many ways things have improved so much for the better, but...I do.

Corfu was calling us now. The children loved it and we loved it too. The next few years we would go to the travel agents, pick up the latest Greek brochures and drool over all the different Greek Islands before focussing on Corfu. There was so much choice on Corfu unlike many of the Mediterranean Islands. Majorca, Minorca and Ibiza are beautiful Islands but there only a handful of resorts to choose from. Corfu has over twenty resorts and they are all different. My favourite brochures were Manos, the Greek travel company and . I used to take their brochure everywhere with me in my lunch bag. At any opportunity I would delve into my bag and browse through the pages for weeks on end. One by one I would read the descriptions and memorise every photo until I knew every apartment in every resort on the Island. Maybe I should have been a travel agent? Well, after a few years the introduction of the flight only option to Corfu was a bonus. We could now book a flight and stay anywhere on the Island and if we wanted to stay a few days in one resort and a few days somewhere else then it was possible. The flights weren't cheap by any means but if you knew a few Greeks with accommodation then the cost was similar and you could choose your own tailor made holiday. This was independent travelling and we liked it.

3. Buying a property on Corfu.

I had always wanted to buy a property in Greece as soon as I arrived on my first visit to Corfu. I had been to Zante on two holidays before I was married so I knew what to expect in terms of the beauty of the Islands. I had been to Ioannina on the mainland and been to the Vikos gorge. I had stayed a few days in Kalambaka and marvelled the great monasteries of Meteora. I had read all the well known books from Corfu, the Greek Islands and the Mainland. I had studied the Greek language at college for two years and had learnt the Greek alphabet, how to read and write Greek. I had read the Odyssey and Homer's Iliad. Now it was time to put some roots down in the Ionian area that we all loved so much. Would we but something in Paxos, Parga or Corfu?

Money was always an issue when it came to buying a property abroad and we didn't have much spare cash as the children were at school and were growing up fast. Like most families we had to feed them, clothe them and fund them as their needs were greater than ours. Ann was back at work now after nine years of raising the children and we both had good jobs. I had my own menswear shop and Ann was a PA to a director at an insurance company. So, could we afford to take on a second mortgage or would it be just a pipe dream?

Paxos was the first place we thought about buying somewhere. A derelict old house and re building it over the next few decades. But we would have to fly to Corfu and take the ferry down or fly to Preveza on the mainland. No, too inaccessible.

 Parga was the second place we looked at but again we were always thinking that if we did buy there, how would we be able to go to Corfu?

Corfu was the easier option and having such a varied amount of resorts and villages to choose from how could we resist?

The Internet was now up and running and we had access to the whole world. I had a laptop at work and could look at all the properties for sale on Corfu in between my daily duties and serving customers. Again after a few weeks I knew all the property agents, all the properties and all the places that we couldn't afford. But I loved to surf the net and every night I would go to bed and dream of owning a beach apartment on Glyfada or Gouvia bay. I used to log on to the Agni forum website and ask questions about how is life on Corfu? What is the weather like and what is happening over there today? I loved it and would check every hour for a response to my questions. I would read and dissect every answer that was posted and loved to hear the members stories whether they lived in Corfu or not.

In 2004 my beloved father, confident and dear friend passed away. This was a dark day and for those of you that have lost a parent that you are close to it is a very sad time. I am one of four children with Judi the oldest, Jacquie was next and then me. Mark was our younger brother. Dad left us a some money in his will and although it wasn't a great deal as it was to be equally split between four of us it got me thinking. Could we now afford to buy a simple place on Corfu? I signed up to a couple of property agents on Corfu to receive their monthly newsletter and continued to trawl their websites to see what we could afford. Well it wasn't much to be honest. Most of the houses within our budget were old delapidated buildings in villages I had never heard of. But it was nice to dream and discuss the possibilities of buying a project.

I bought the excellent hand drawn map of Corfu by Stefan and would pinpoint where on the Island these properties were. This knowledge would come in handy at a later date when I decided to write a book about the history of the Corfu villages. Then one day I had newsletter email from Corfu property agency. There were several new properties on the list and one in particular caught my eye. One bedroom apartment for sale in Perama. I liked the look of this one as it was one of five in a newly renovated two story block. There were plenty of photos so I printed them off and put them in a A4 binder and off I went to show Ann at home. The bedroom was a good size and had two single beds. The walls were painted white and the furniture consisted of a wardrobe, dressing table and bedside tables all in pine. The bed linen and matching curtains were shades of light and dark blue. There was a separate kitchen with a cooker and fridge installed and a table and chairs in pine with again matching table cloth and curtains in shades of blue. The view from the balcony looked over the sea and there was a beach just over the main road where it was situated. The lady who had re-furbished the building had a good eye for detail and we liked it so much we contacted the agents and agreed to a 10% deposit pending a viewing and a meeting with a Greek solicitor.

We arrived on Corfu in May 2005 and had arranged to meet with the agents in Corfu town for a chat before heading down town to meet with the solicitor. The meeting with the agents went well and then we walked down to see our solicitor. Arthouros Zervos was a tall handsome man dressed in a grey suit with a matching shirt and tie and he spoke very good English which was good. He showed us the plans and then asked us to sit down. He pointed out to us that the apartment was illegal and the developer did not have planning permission. The five apartments were made from the original building but it was owned by a single person. The developers plan was to sell five apartments to five owners but you would need a lot more land than what was there. So, Arthorous said. You can buy it but... if the law changes you will be subject to any planning fines and if you want to sell it you will have to inform the buyer that it is illegal too. I asked him if he thought we should buy it knowing that there were many illegal buildings on Corfu and his reply was

No! So, that was it. Our first dream shattered and we hadn't even been to view the property, there was no point now. In recent times the Greek government has imposed fines for all illegal buildings, extensions and swimming pools. So in hind site it was the right decision.

Another summer over and the search continued online through September and October. In November I saw a property that said there were two double bedroom and two single bedroom apartment for sale on the ground floor in a new development with a further five apartments on the second floor with upper floor bedrooms. There were only a couple of photographs to see. One was of the building itself and one was of the view from the downstairs balcony. The second photograph showed a large swimming pool in the foreground and a view over the green clad valley to Corfu town and the sea. In the distance was the Greek mainland and mountains. The price of the double apartments were a fair price but we would have had to borrow money to top up what dad had left by way of a mortgage. It was very tempting but on further inspection and on page two of the advert there was a description of the one bedroom apartment. One of the two had already been sold and the other one was available. I couldn't wait to get home and tell Ann, we could afford to buy this one. The next day I emailed the agency and told them that I would be sending a 10% deposit for the single apartment. They asked me if I would like to wait until the following May to view the property first. I said no, I don't need to as I know exactly where it is. It was in the olive groves on the side of the hill to the village of Pelekas. I had already been to Pelekas beach (Kontogialos) on my first visit to Dassia all those years ago and knew what a beautiful sandy beach it was. I had only ever driven through the village of Pelekas itself on the way to Glyfada but I remember seeing a few tavernas and a couple of bars so that will do for us.

The following May 2006 we stayed in Agios Gordios as it was close to Pelekas and we arranged to see the apartment with the project manager Antoine who was a Dutchman who owned a villa nearby on the Kokkini road. We were pleased with what we saw. The view was indeed more beautiful than we could have imagined. To the left was the mighty Pantokrator mountain, the highest of the mountains on Corfu. Further round we could see as far as the Barbati headland and with binoculars the Albainian town of Saranda. Looking over the valley we could see the village of Afra and Mandouki, the sea and mainland Greece. Straight ahead was Corfu town and to the right the second highest mountain on Corfu, Agioi Deka. Which means ten saints.

We had a small grassed garden. A walk up half a dozen metal steps to the balcony. Double slatted door shutters painted green and a double glass door led us into the bedroom. A separate bathroom and kitchen lay further ahead and to the front door also painted in green. On the front door was the number three. That would be our new address when we came next year once all the development was finished and we were ready to move in. We paid the balance on the apartment and the sale went through without any problems. And it was legal! Number 3, Olive Grove, Pelekas, Corfu.

In May 2007 the apartment was finished so my brother in law, Kenny and I headed out for a week with the mission of making the apartment habitable for the pending family holiday in August. We decided to stay at Alexandros rooms above the taverna in the village. We hired a car so that we could buy all the necessary kitchen and dining ware that would be needed for a comfortable stay. A week earlier I had arranged the transport from our English address to the Pelekas address, a double bed, wardrobe, dressing table, kitchen table and chairs. The rest of the items we needed would be bought locally on Corfu. Dave Jackson was the man who picked up the furniture from our house in England and on this trip he had decided to drive a big truck to Corfu instead of his usual white transit van. His trip was flawed from the start. There are several check points in different countries on the way to Corfu and Dave got fined a few times for being over weight. When he dropped our stuff off he reversed the lorry into a wall, smashed the back lights and damaged the bodywork. I don't think he made much money on this trip.

Once the apartment was clean we could assemble all of the flat pack furniture and check the list to see what we needed to buy. Working during the day and staying in the village was a good idea as we got to meet all the taverna and bar owners. They had plenty of time for us as it was the first week in May and many of them had just opened for the season. We asked lots of questions and they gave us all the answers. We bought a lot of what we needed from the Profi store at Alykes Potamou. Two heavy plastic sun loungers, lounger covers, a large plastic table and two chairs for outdoor living. Crockery, cutlery, pots, pans, frying pan, washing up bowl, drainer, kettle, table cloths etc. In fact everything you would need to kit out a lounge, kitchen, bedroom and bathroom. If we could find it, we bought it. Now I said to Kenny, How the hell are we going to get all this into the small car we have hired?

I wish we could have taken selfies back then. We had the boot open with the sun loungers hanging out the back. Even with the back seats down the car was absolutely packed. The girl on the till had helped us carry some of the goods to the car and she was astonished to see how much we had bought and asked how we were going to get it all back to Pelekas. She was even more astonished as we drove off with everything wedged in and burst out laughing when I turned out of the car park and the window wipers turned on because the sun loungers were above our heads and we couldn't move. And the wipers continued to turn themselves on every single right hand turn all the way home.

For the next few years we would enjoy holidaying in Pelekas and blending into village life. We had Greek neighbours in the house next door and also down the hill at the bottom of our land and the car park. Then their were our neighbours from the apartment who were a mixture from different countries.

Next door lived Spiros the long distance lorry driver and his wife Alexandria who was from a Greek mainland village. They had the most adorable small dog named Hera. She was what looked like a cross between a German dachshund and a Jack Russel with short red hair. Whenever we were there she would climb through a hole in the wire boundary fence and join us at the dinner table or down by the pool. When Bobby swam around the pool Hera would chase after him from the poolside.

The neighbours down the bottom were Christos the father and his two sons Stamatis and Gerasimos. We have got to know them very well over the years and we often find a bottle of home made red wine on the patio after we have arrived. The sons who are in their late twenties own the Pelekas Café in the village.

On the ground floor of the apartment if you stand facing it from the gardens are four apartments. The one on the left is a one bedroom apartment owned by a Dutch couple, Antoine and Kate Creemers. They have a house on the Kokkini road and wanted the extra rooms for visiting family and for the swimming pool as they have three young boys. Antoine was the project manager for the renovation of the building and gave us a lot of useful information before and after we moved in.

The next apartment is a double and the couple are from Ioannina on the mainland. Kostas Kaputsides is an English teacher and his wife Valya is an Ancient Greek language teacher from Volos. They have two children, Zizis and Demitria. They are similar ages to Eva and Bobby so that was a good thing when we played games in the pool or had a family BBQ together.

The next apartment is ours, then next door to the right is Dimitris Athansiou. Dimi as we call him is from Athens but grew up on Corfu in Mandouki by the port. Like so many Greek families over the past years, his mother and father left Corfu to find work in Athens. His parents, Andreas as Vaso stay sometimes which Dimi doesn't like too much but I do as if I am on my own for a week or so Vaso will always make me a beautiful Greek dinner...everyday! Dimi and his father look after all of our electricity and water bills. The maintenance on the gardens, car park and the swimming pool. He sends out emails of what the yearly charges will be and I work as a go between if there are any issues. This year for instance we had one side of the building tiled and the front side painted in Corfu yellow. The bill was split between nine owners so not too expensive and the building is looking new again.

Steps lead up to the second floor where there are five apartments with the lounge, kitchen and bathroom on the ground floor and a large bedroom upstairs. A Dutch lady and her Swedish partner live on the top left hand side. We have known Ciska since the day we moved in and have had many a good night in Pelekas. Eirik is a new addition to the Pelekas family and knows Pelekas very well from previous holidays to the village.

As I write this I don't know the people who own the next apartment as it was empty for a few years following a legal dispute but I'm sure we will get to know them once they start to visit.

Above our place is and English lady and her Australian husband. Kate and Kim have three children, two boys and a girl. Michael owns the next one along. He is a Czech born Canadian who bought the place to rent out so we don't see him very often. The owners of the last apartment on the right hand side are a couple from Ireland, Joe and Kelly.

Luckily we get on with all our neighbours but having said that it depends on what time of year we go as to who we see there. In the early years we went in the school holidays so we saw more of Ciska, Dimitris, Kostas and Valya. In recent times although there are nine apartments we are often the only ones there. Either way there is always a warm welcome from our Greek neighbours who live nearby or from anyone who is at the apartments.

Having now bought a place of our own the temptation to visit more than in May and August when the children had their school holidays. We wouldn't be tied to May and August anymore so my plan was to visit for the Greek Easter.

In 2011 the Greek Easter was at the end of April. We booked our flights and was pleased that it was a different date to the English Easter so the flight prices were reasonable. I flew out a week before as I had a few things to do before the family arrived. I had decided to buy a scooter in the August the previous year so that if we needed anything from the village or if we had to go to town for anything we wouldn't have to rely on the infrequent bus service. Although the bus service is always on time it would give us some independence. If you remember the story about when Kenny and I filled the car with household goods then I can beat that with the scooter.

I made the short journey towards Corfu town and stopped at the Diellas shop near Potomos. I had to buy food and drinks for when the family arrived and unlike in previous years where we would hire a car for a few days or a week to do the shopping and go sightseeing this time I would use the new scooter.

I bought all the usual stuff for breakfast and lunch, then a few things for the odd evening meal as we would eat out a few nights a week too. So armed with a back pack I bought the breakfast items consisting of bacon, eggs, bread for toast, butter, milk, orange juice and six bottles of water. For our lunch on the balcony or on a table by the swimming pool I bought ham, lettuce, tomatoes, onions, cucumber, feta cheese, olives and some oregano. For evening meals I just bought some potatoes, fresh chicken breasts, minced beef and some pork souvlaki for the outside BBQ. Also, twenty four cans of Greek beer a large container of red village wine and some toilet and kitchen roll. Feeling pleased with myself and looking forward to eating proper meals at home I carried the bags of food out to the scooter. Wow! There was a lot of food and drink here so I put the heavier stuff under the seat, the pack of beer and the bottles of water in the foot well and the rest in the ruck sack which was extremely heavy but when it was on my back I could rest it on the back seat where Ann would usually sit. I drove next door to Profi and picked up some tobacco from the "Periptero" Kiosk from the roadside. We needed a step ladder, a mirror and a fan. Once I had bought these I had to figure out how to fit them on to the scooter. Again the assistant looked at me as if I was crazy buying all of these things and came outside to help me load up. I had the step ladder in front of me and the mirror wedged in between my legs but there was no room for error as I headed back to Pelekas. On the way back I went around the Afra roundabout and noticed a flower shop on the right hand side. I stopped the scooter and asked if they had a red Geranium and a pack of compost. The man recognised me from a previous visit when I had bought a garden turf for three of the gardens for the apartments. When I ordered the turf the year before I had measured the gardens and walked in armed with all the measurements only for him to tell me that they would send someone out to measure and the turf would be imported from Athens and delivered the following week. He said are you crazy "Malaka" Where will you put these thing you want to buy? I said just put the compost on top of the beer and bottles of water and the Geranium on the handlebars? So, I headed for home with a heavy back pack, a full under seat, foot well and handlebars. I was positioned upright and my legs were out at the side of the scooter. I could hardly reach the handlebars which was a small problem as I definitely couldn't reach the brake. When I reached the apartment I shouted to Ciska who was luckily sunbathing by the pool to come and help me unload. Quickly! It was risky but I got away with it and the very next day I saw Dimitris the taxi driver on a scooter in the village with his wife and daughter on the back and his son and the dog in the front. This is Corfu!

Chapter 4. Corfu Central.

The idea for the eBook about the Corfu villages came about when I was asked to be a moderator for the Travel and Tourism section for an online Corfu forum which was launched in January 2012.

Having written the sections for "Corfu resorts" "Out and about" and "Holiday reports" I proceeded to write a section for the Corfu villages. It was then that I realised how little information and photographs there were on the internet. I searched a minimum of ten pages on search engines for each village with mixed results. I searched through travel sites, guides and blogs. I then looked for books about the villages and there were none. So, there was the challenge, I would have to use what little information I had gained from the internet, visit the villages myself and take my own photographs to compile enough information to write a book.

Luckily I had been going to Corfu for over 25 years and had already visited some of the villages to be featured, but, I decided to visit them all with a fresh outlook. I had four holidays booked for the season, cheap flights were bought and as we own a small apartment in the village of Pelekas, it wouldn't be too costly.

I set myself a target for the year and once in Corfu set out each day on my scooter to each village. It was then I realised just how big Corfu is. It is for this reason that I decided to write the book in three stages. The first book will be about the central Corfu Villages. The second and third will be about the villages of the North and the villages of the South.

When you drive 20 kilometres to a village in the mountains it's not as simple as you think. Climbing several hundred meters high up narrow zig zag roads to reach your destination is very tiring. But, when you reach the village it is all worth while as the views of the island are simply spectacular and everyone different.

All the villages in the book have their own story to tell. They are all unique for some reason or another whether it be for their history, landmarks, local traditions or views. Each one has been visited and photographed by me and each one that was chosen had to meet certain criteria so that the visitor would enjoy their trip to the hidden wonders of the real Corfu as it has remained for centuries.

As I have spent so many happy and memorable times in Corfu I thought it was time to give something back to the island. Writing the book gave me that opportunity and I intended to give all of the profits to the charities and villages of Corfu. I would like to thank you for buying the book and all of the people who have helped and supported me throughout, you know who you are.

When I was writing the Central part of Corfu villages book I headed for the village of Varypatades near Pelekas. As I rode up through the olive groves to the villages I had my doubts if this village would make the final 50 villages to make the book. There is not much history to the village and only has a small population. The yearly panigiri is the biggest event of the year, there are no shops as the minimarket closed down and the only kafeneion opens for the locals around 7.30...sometimes!

So, what was it about this village that impressed me to include it in the book? Well, as I approached the village, I could see Pelekas in the distance on my right hand side so I stopped to take a photograph. A little further on through the narrow winding streets bordered with white painted lines I arrived at the centre. There was a small square with a church and some green iron benches. I parked the scooter and walked up to the two old ladies and the old gentleman and was a little nervous. They were surprised to see me and we talked in Greek about the village as they could not speak English. I must have used every Greek word that I knew to ask the questions I needed if the village was to be included. When is the panigiri? What is the name of the church? Who is the Saint? How many people live here? etc...The ladies were dressed in a simple skirt and blouse with a cardigan and the man was dressed in trousers and a long sleeved shirt and were all in their 80's. There was a lot of laughing and a lot of missing teeth! They told me to walk up to the top of the village where the main church is and you can see both sides of the Island. What a view! I thanked them on the way back down and as I rode through the olives I saw a 2 feet long Balkan lizard dressed in lime green. As I turned the corner I yelled out loud...Aghhh, this Island is Fantastic!!! Well I swore actually...In the book I describe Varypatades as, "The Sun always shines on Varypatades" Because from Pelekas it always catches the sun until the late evening when everywhere else around the area has lost it. That was one of my fondest memories when visiting the villages and a true "Euphoria moment"

At the end of the summer season I would have enough photographs and information to release an eBook about the Corfu central region and start raising some money for food for the poorer families on Corfu as the crisis was biting hard. I had asked around Pelekas if families were finding it difficult to make ends meet and how they were coping in the villages around the area. I was told that many people were struggling to get by and that a couple of soup kitchen's had been set up in Corfu town and that Greek the Red cross were taking donations from those that could spare a little food. So I had the idea to write a book and I had a worthy cause to drive me on my mission.

It would take three years to complete the three eBooks about the three areas of Corfu. At the end of the third year I would release a Corfu villages printed book which would contain all fifty villages and hopefully it would sell well so I could make a real difference.

My first visit to Corfu was in May 2012. I took one of the first flights from Manchester as I was eager to get started on the book and I was very excited at the prospect of travelling around the different villages. I had a one week holiday so I would have to go out for at least five of those days. If I could cover five or more villages on this trip then I was sure I would be able to reach the eighteen to twenty I wanted by the end of the season and I had two more visits to come.

I set off on my first expedition on my new scooter armed with my trusted map which I had bought from the Agni forum by Stefan Jaskulowski. Stefan had released this book in 1997 and he travelled the Island extensively as he was tired of using the basic Corfu maps which were in many areas completely inaccurate. His map is hand drawn and written and in my opinion is still the best map of Corfu. I would need this as I didn't want to end up going down a country road and coming to a dead end like Stefan had done on many occasions before he researched his map.

My first port of call was the village of Vatos on the central west coast so not far from Pelekas. I arrived in the main square and took some photographs. There was a small shop but there was nobody around to ask any questions about the history of the village. A friend of mine had agreed to come with me on this my first day out and he knew the village quite well. Domonic said he would show me where the church was and then we would go down to nearby Kelia where there is a taverna and shop called "Spiros 97". They have had a family business there for over sixty years and they would be able to help me with the history of the area.

Vatos.

Vatos is a small, quiet village in the central west area of the island; about 20 kilometres from Corfu town. There are a couple of tavernas, a church, a café and a shop. Next door to Kelia, it has probably one of the best tavernas in the area. It was famous for camping in the 1980s when, like Pelekas, young people came from Europe, America and Australasia to visit the new place to be. Located on a hilltop, Vatos is only a few minutes drive from famous beaches of Corfu; such as Ermones, Pelekas, Glyfada and Myrtiotissa.

The lush green valley around Vatos was actually once a huge lake. Ropa valley, as it is called, covers an area of 10km² and extends all over central west Corfu. This vast meadow where herds of sheep graze is rich with olive trees and vineyards. River Ermones crosses the valley, forming lovely lakes. The region constitutes an important life reserve, the hospitable refuge for various species of birds, fish, amphibians and reptiles. Exploring the area by car, bike or on foot is well worth the effort.

The village was once the residence of the area's two most prominent lords Kapodistrias and Soufis, but unfortunately only a small part of the old mansion is preserved today. The village festival takes place on 24th September, and on this date in nearby Mirtiotissa a celebration is held at the monastery of Panagia Myrtiotissa.   The valley below also hosts the Corfu golf club. An 18-hole golf course and driving range near Ermones. The tree lined fairways and the sand bunkers are combined with several lakes and streams, one of which flows to the beach at Ermones where Odysseus was rescued by princess Nafsika. The course is very picturesque against the backdrop of high hills viewed on all sides. A magical place full of animals and birds, fish, kingfishers, herons and otters.

This was a great place to start and I jotted down all the information the mother and father gave me and together with my own research I was pleased with my first work. I had taken the photographs with a Sony instamatic camera which was up to the job and I was helped by the fact that the light on Corfu is so good. I thanked Domonic and when I got home I quickly loaded the images on to my Microsoft Surface as a back up. I had a rest, then a shower and then settled down on the patio with a glass of village red wine. I must have looked at the photographs a hundred times before going up to the village for something to eat and a few well earned beers. It had been a good day but the next few days would be different. I would be on my own and I would have to travel further than Vatos which was only down the road.

On the second day I had planned to go further up the west coast to Giannades, Marmaro and Kanakades. The three villages were quite close together and I could take the country road which would take over the plain of the Ropa valley. If I could visit three villages in a day it would be a bonus and take some of the pressure off which I had put myself under. I arrived in the square in Giannades and parked the scooter outside the café. I bought a hot coffee and sat on the metal benches to admire the view over the green hills and the valley below. I walked up to the church and recognised the Greek saint's name and the date that it was built. I made some notes and looked at the map to see where I would go next. I was enjoying this and thought to myself, I would like to do this for a job.

Giannades.

Giannades is situated in the central west area of Corfu, connected with the national road to Paleokastrista. Corfu Town is 20 kilometres away and the nearest resort is Ermones. The population is around 760 and agriculture is the main income here.

Giannades is a quiet village frequented by artists for its secluded spot. There is a butcher, a bakery, post office, medical help, mini markets, restaurants, a bar, a school, kindergarden and a theatre. Although not all are open all year round.

The Church here is devoted to Saint Nicholas and is accessed by several steps upward and through an arched gateway. To the left you can view the well kept cemetery with it's white marble epitaphs that sit below the wall.

You can also buy fresh fish and vegetables from the merchants; who pass by daily with their trucks, announcing their arrival with their loudspeakers.

Giannades village has his own secret beach named Yali. It is a small bay just behind the hill, which is reachable by a path or by boat. But don't tell anyone….it's a secret.

Although only 150 metres high on a hill the views from the square overlooking the Ropa Valley are beautiful. You can sit on a large raised amphitheatre like area made of stone and drink a Greek cup of coffee from the café behind you.

Across the road is a tap where you can fill up your bottle with fresh mountain water before heading off to the next village.

The short drive bought me to the small village of Marmaro. It was midday now and it was getting hot. The village houses were somewhat rundown but it a certain charm. I found the village church and sat down for cigarette break. It was very quiet now and most of the villagers had settled down for an afternoon siesta. I didn't find anyone to talk here to so I would have to work hard to find out about the history about the village from some of my Greek friends.

Marmaro.

Marmaro, meaning Marble in Greek, is a small village and lies in the hills on the western side of Corfu. The first settlers, in post Byzantine times, were pirates who had fled the armies of the empire and became fugitives. They made makeshift settlements in the inaccessible areas above the Ropa Valley. Around 1783 the villagers lived under a Venetian feudal lord Marco

Marcello. They cultivated the land for the lord and lived in poverty.

The architecture is unusual for Corfu as the use of marble can be seen at the church and around arched doorways.

The church here is called Aghia Marina. Dating back to 1630, its foundation is celebrated on the 17th July. Two other churches were built sometime later but the church of Saint John is now a convent and the church of Saint Panteleimon was sacked and destroyed by pirates.

As you enter the village you can easily miss the very old arched bridge, which was built centuries ago. It wasn't for a while until I realised where the bridge was. I had taken a photograph on the main road opposite the church and noticed I was standing on it.

The kafenion serves the local villagers and any strangers that happen to walk by. There is no tourism in Marmaro: it is a very simple place which hasn't change much in centuries. This is a great place to practice your Greek, as many of the people I met spoke very little English.

Kanakades.

I parked before the village of Kanakades because I had been told that the road was narrow and in the late afternoon people would be sleeping and the noise of the scooter would be intrusive. I saw the church straight away as I walked up the hill to the platia (Centre). My first impression was that it would be another plain building as my first view was from the side wall. As I turned the corner I was amazed at what I saw next. The frontage to the church was beautifully hand painted either side of the doorway with images of the patron saint. There was a car park for about ten cars so I could of driven up as it was only the first week of May but I wasn't to know that at the time. The village had a mixture of houses, old and new.

As you drive up the hill to the village look to the left and you will see the ruins of an old fortress which is where the baroness Marcello lived and ruled during the Venetian occupation.

Marcello ruled nearly all of the Ropa valley area and made huge demands on the tenant farmers who would donate "givings" of the crops that they grew. Grain, grapes and olives were all handed over as a form of tax or rent for the protection she gave them.

The descendants of the Marcello family can still be found in Venice to this day. Although the building was given back to the Greek state in the second world war.

The municipality of Parelion bought it afterwards, planning to restore it and turn it into a centre for traditional Corfiot cuisine.

The view from the old mansion to the Ropa Valley and the hills are wonderful, taking in the Ropa valley and hills beyond.

As you walk into the small village square, look to your left and you will see the façade and doorway to the church of saint Catherine. The doors have pillars either side the saints are beautifully painted on the entrance walls.

The artwork on the facia is truly stunning and is the best I have ever seen. I could sit outside the kafeneion here, drink an ouzo and gaze around the pretty multi coloured houses for hours.

I was hungry now and decided to head back to Pelekas. When I got back I was quite tired. I needed to speak to someone who spoke English, I was Greeked out.

I was ahead of schedule but for a village to be included in the book it would have to be worth visiting so, when I had compiled all the information it wasn't a foregone conclusion that the village I had been to would be used.

The villages I had been to so far had all been lovely in their own way. They were all different and had their own character. How would I choose the final fifty villages when it came to it? Would I upset anyone whose village was not in the book? Would they buy the book if their village was not in it? I didn't know but I had to follow my own instincts and go with my gut feelings. At the end of the day I am not an author of books, a historian or a travel expert. I just want to raise money for the poorer people of my favourite Island.

In Pelekas, the taverna, bar owners and villagers would ask how I was getting on with my research and would ask me where I had been that day. I would tell them what I had seen, you I had spoken to and would show them the photographs. I would be surprised when many of them would say, "That looks nice, I have never been there". They showed a great interest and when I explained why I was writing a book they were genuinely supportive which spurred me on to reach my goal.

The next day I had a big breakfast at home and made a flask of coffee for my trip to Liapades, Lakones and Doukades. This would be the furthest I had been so far but I knew that I would be able to have lunch in a taverna as these three villages were bigger than the ones I had been to so far.

I took the Paleokastritsa road this time as it is a main road and I needed to go a fair distance. Liapades was nice and I popped into one of the three kafenion's to ask about the village. It was a nice surprise as the lady was from Liverpool and had married a Greek man from the village.

Liapades.

"A House in Corfu" is a book written by Emma Tennant. It tells the story of her parents who, whilst on a cruise in the early 1960's, saw a remote bay near Liapades on the west coast of Corfu. They decided to build a house there, in an area we know today as Rovinia. It is set in 42 hectares of land above the bay where legend has it Ulysses was shipwrecked and found by Nausicaa, daughter of King Alcinous.

Liapades village sits high on the side of a hill about 20 kilometres north west of

Corfu town and near to the resort of Paleokastritsa. A 1km walk downhill will take you to Liapades beach; where there are plenty of shops and tavernas and a horseshoe shaped pebble beach known locally as Gefira (meaning bridge in Greek). There are as many as 15 small coves nearby: some can be reached through dense paths, while others are only accessible by boat.

With a population of around one thousand, the village has a reputation for producing a fine wine from the grape variety called "kakotrigis". The name Liapades derives from the word "Aliplakti" which means sea-beaten.

 The first settlers came from Alpia, a part of the Paleokastritsa region, who moved to the current location to avoid being seen by pirates from the sea.

Alipa over time became Liapades or Alipades.

The main church is saint Anastasia which was built around 1600 to 1630 and has been fully restored to its original state. It is well worth visiting this church to see its painted ceiling and icons. The village festival is held on 14th August in honour of Maria Ascension. The surrounding area is a walkers paradise with great views and has a Corfu trail starting point.

Lakones.

Lakones was next on the list and I had been here many times before on the way to see the beautiful views from the "Bella Vista" hotel and the viewpoint. There are traffic lights here and there is a sign as you stop at the red light. It says "Change of lights 7 minutes and 30 seconds" This is a beautiful village with amazing views over the bays of Paleokastritsa and the monastery below.

Paleokastritsa's coastline with small bays and coves have been viewed by many travellers, over the years, from the village in the hills above. This is the village of Lakones, from which you can best enjoy the landscape of the region. Looking down to the crystal clear waters below and contours of the coastline is a truly breath taking view.

In summer there are traffic lights operating on the main road through the village; as the road is so narrow in parts, you wouldn't want to squeeze past an oncoming car. Believe me: I have done it. There are a couple of great tavernas here and the church of saint Nicholas stands proud in the square for the 500 residents. The name Lakones probably originates from the displacement of people from the mainland (Sparta is the capital of Lakonia). As you come up the winding road from Paleokastritsa, look for a left hand turn to Lakones. The upwards leading, snaking road will take you to the village. You can stop just short if it and walk around the streets. Afterwards, drive through and stop at Bella Vista: its name says it all.

Every day dozens of tourists gather on the balconies of the rented rooms and in the tavernas to admire the unique panorama. Telescopes are permanently installed on open, flat areas to help you enjoy the view in more detail. In my opinion this is one of the best views in the Mediterranean.

The village itself, with its narrow, well kept streets and Venetian houses, is just as pretty as the view. You can also walk to Paleokastritsa along the path, which is lined with pine trees. If you are around the west coast then you must surely visit Lakones. I think it will give you the inspiration to visit more of Corfu's beautiful and varied villages.

I drove inland next to the village of Doukades where I had lunch. This is a busy village with three excellent tavernas. The history was very interesting and my lunch was very good. When I arrived back in Pelekas I just fell on the bed and dozed off for an hour. This village malarkey was hard work, but well worth it.

Doukades.

If you could visit just one of the villages of Corfu island, then you would certainly choose Doukades. The village is around 20 kilometres north west of Corfu town on the road to Paleokastritsa.

The village is first mentioned in a notary act of 1616. The name of the village, according to some researchers, derived from its first residents; who all had the surname Doukas. It is set out like an amphitheatre on the hillside; with its Venetian stone houses, picturesque square and the neo-classical style primary school. As you approach the village, park your car in the car park and set off to roam the narrow streets, admiring the colours of the Venetian houses and the carved stone walls with their wooden doorways.

At the entrance of the village there is a street with amazing panoramic view, which will take you to the hill of Agia Anna 2km walk, where there is a café, or to the isolated chapel of Ai Simios which is 1km walk. The most famous building in the village is the house of Georgios Theotokis, a descendant of the great family of politicians. Work on the mansion began in 1900, when Theotokis was prime minister. The house was abandoned after the last war but is now being renovated to house a library of political science, with accommodation for researchers who come to study the rich family archives.

There is the church of Yperageia Theotokos , a mini market, a butcher and three tavernas in the small square. So you are sure to eat fresh meat and if you are lucky, it may have been blessed.

Before you leave Doukades enjoy the village pastitsada, one of the best in Corfu, served at Elizabetta's taverna in the village square.

In three days I had photographed seven villages and taken notes in preparation to write the history of them when I got back to the UK. I was very pleased and decided to spend the next few days as a tourist should by going to the beach and popping into Corfu town.

I had a couple of months before my return to Corfu so I worked on the book and asked an internet friend of mine who built the website for my menswear shop to set up a separate website for the Corfu villages. Leon gave me a good price and did a lot of the work for free as it was for charity. Another friend of mine who is a graphic designer said that he would design the book and prepare it for release on the website and on the Amazon bookstore. So, everything was in place to launch the book and raise some money later in the year. All I had to do was go to Corfu and supply all of the material.

It was August when I returned to the Emerald Isle and I was looking forward to a two week holiday. It would be a mixture of work and play as I would have to visit at least ten villages on this visit. On the list this time was Kinopiastes, Kastellani mesi and Kouramades. These villages are quite close together so I could go to all three in one day. The nearby villages to Pelekas of Agios Ioannis, Sinarades, Varipatades and Kokkini was again an easy day out. A longer drive to the northern boundary of the central region would include Kato Korakiana and Ano Korakiana. The village of Kompitsi could be visited on the way to Corfu town and so could Gastouri. That would leave only a few villages left for my October holiday and the pressure would be off to complete the first book. I decided that I would go to the villages every other day this time as going out everyday in May was very tiring, especially on a scooter.

I have a friend called Lavinia Psarras who lives in Kinopiastes and the first time I went to visit her she told me that the views as you descend from the top of the hill coming from Pelekas are beautiful. I reached the top of the hill after Agios Proskopis and started my descent down the snaking bends of the valley. When I got half way down I saw exactly what Vinny, as I call her, had described to me in the winter the year before. I parked the scooter on a bend half way down the road. What lay before me was the most stunning garden of greenery I had ever seen. It was a huge area on the side of a mountain covered with olive groves and peppered with scores of dark green Cypress trees. The olive trees swayed in the breeze showing their different shades of light green and silver. The Cypress trees stood tall like soldiers on duty and in the sunshine took on a blue hue which cast a sharp contrast to the trees nearby. As I gazed up to the top of the mountain the sun blinded me with its bright orb in the heat of midday. This is still one of my favourite places to stop for a break when I am travelling to the south of the Island. It is truly a hidden treasure and can go unnoticed as there is nowhere to park your car as it is a tight bend on a busy road.

Kinopiastes.

The traditional village of Kinopiastes in the Messi region of Corfu is only 10 kilometres southwest from Corfu town and the airport.

Old mansions of the 17th to 19th centuries, a marble church, a 17th century monastery and some of the most famous restaurants on the island, are all good reasons to visit this village. Another good reason is the island's only Museum, devoted to the olive tree.

Music is a great tradition of the village and they have a very good philharmoniki (brass band), as well as a wonderful church choir. In the height of summer there are often concerts held in the square and the festival, held on august 15th, sees the village full to capacity with almost 1300 residents.

The Tripas taverna has been visited by former Greek president Constantine Karamanlis, French president Francois Mitterand, actor Anthony Quinn, actress Jane Fonda and Aristotle Onassis, to name just a few.

The main church is devoted to the Virgin Mary and it is in the central square. It is a traditional church with unique architecture and an impressive marble entrance. Inside, there are frescoes of the 18th century Ionian school of painting.

This is a well kept and beautifully painted village which also has a mini market and a café where I was amazed to buy a frappe for 1.50 euros.

The villages of Kastellani mesi, Kouramades and Kokkini were lovely in their own way but when it came to choosing the final twenty to be included in the book unfortunately these three would not be added.

I remember a conversation I had one evening in Agios Ioannis as we sat under the big tree at the taverna. I asked a local man how much he thought the old mansion was worth. He said the owner would take nothing less than one million euros for it. I said that because it was in disrepair and it needed a lot of work and money spending on it there was no way it was worth that price. Yes he said, but, the owner is a millionaire in the village if he doesn't sell it isn't he?

Agios Ioannis.

In the heart of the Island just 10 kilometres west of Corfu Town is the village of Agios Ioannis. It has a taverna in the square and a nice Church.

Agios Ioannis was one of the first places the backpackers found over 30 years ago who set up their tents amid the olive groves in what is still known today as 'The Cactus Hilton'. The village itself is next door to the mighty Aqualand Water Park and hardly gets a mention in it's own right. There is a taverna in the main square where you can sit in the shade under the old Plane Tree. The Church of Saint John is next door and opposite is a Hotel which was once the village mansion.

It is most famous in modern times for the staging of the yearly Agiofest Rock Music Festival where bands from all over the world come to perform. Since 2009 this event has been held in the olive and orange groves and takes place around the end of August.

My family and twelve Dutch people went to the taverna one night and we sat on white plastic chairs lined with long white plastic tables. The Lady of the house served us and the gentleman of the house cooked the meals. We had a great night out and the service was fantastic. The bizarre thing about it was, when we ordered our starters, let's say Tzatski, Calamari and Greek salad etc. Everyone's Tzatsiki was served first, then all the Calamari, then all the Greek salads? By the time the last starters were served then the main meals were arriving. It wasn't until later that we realised that the lady was serving everyone and the husband was cooking all of the meals. By the end of the night though, the taverna was packed and we all got fed and watered. It was a great night.

We had stayed in Agios Gordios many times but I had never been to the village of Sinarades before we had bought our place in Pelekas. It is a lovely village and is only down a short distance to drive to from our village. Many of the people who have a business or work in Agios Gordios live in Sinarades. When I visited the main square, which is a round car park surrounded by palm trees, the centre was alive with greenery. I went there recently and was horrified to see that the palms had all but disappeared. The invasion of the palm weevil from Africa has had a catastrophic effect on this species and has wiped out many of the trees on Corfu. You could say that it is ironic really as the palm tree is not indigenous to Corfu but was transported to the Island many years ago.

Sinarades.

Situated 13 kilometres west of Corfu town, Sinarades is built on a hillside covered with olives and almond trees. The water from the mountain springs collects in a small river at the base of the hillside, a river that once divided the village in two. The main occupation of the locals is tourism and farming; the most important products being olive oil, wine, vegetables and fruit. Sinarades comes from the Byzantine surname Sinaras. A cluster of graves scattered around the area dating back to the Roman age have been discovered just one kilometre outside of the village. This discovery indicates that this area might have been an ancient village during the Roman conquest. The village in its current location was built between the 10th and 11th century by the inhabitants of a seashore village, which was abandoned because of the terrible and repeated forays of the Sarakin pirates. Although the village was built earlier, nothing was documented about its existence prior to the 15th century. Stories of incursions by the Turks and Algerians have been handed down from generation to generation. Today Sinarades village numbers 1,200 inhabitants and it caters well for the locals and visitors, providing healthcare facilities such as a community surgery and pharmacy.

The Folklore museum of Sinarades was established in 1982 and is one of the best in Greece. Festival day falls on the Monday after Easter. The 15th of August is Virgin Mary's feast, when the people walk round the village with the icons and banners of the churches ending up at the village square; where a great feast takes place. With its narrow paths, embossed entrances, old houses with small terraces and marble stairs, beautiful churches with high and elegant belfries, with two mansions and the famous folklore museum; Sinarades is one of the biggest and most beautiful villages on Corfu. The nearest resort is the sandy beach at Agios Gordios.

In the hills which are the spine of the central area lies Varypatades. I have already told you of my first visit to this village but I have been back on many occasions since. One day Ann and I made our way down a track from the back streets that led eventually to the Pelekas to Sinarades road. As we reached the ground level we heard the most amazing noise? On further inspection we found a lake with many different species of birds with their young chicks. But what was the deep croaking noise we could hear? We parked the scooter and crept quietly forward to the edge of the lake to find a thousand giant frogs calling out a mating call. As we arrived at the waters edge it went silent. We backed away and the croaking began again. We moved forward and it all went quiet. We could see the frogs and they were huge but it was clear that they didn't want an audience so we continued on our way through the vineyards to the main road.

Varypatades.

"The sun always shines on Varypatades" That is what we say, looking over to the village on the hill from vantage points on the west coast. As the sun goes down Varypatades catches the last rays well into the evening and shines out as a whitewashed beacon; the red dome of the church like a matchstick on standby, to keep the embers glowing.

Half way along the road from Corfu town to Pelekas, on the west coast, is a left hand turn which will take you up a gradual climb to the village. This is a narrow road with what seems like a hundred bends. There is a good size car park where you can leave the car and walk in to the square. The village is a labyrinth of cobbled streets but - unlike in Greek mythology where King Minos kept the Minotaur captive - you won't get lost here.

The houses are beautifully painted and restored and stand side by side with the old houses now deserted and empty. It is a delight to walk around on a hot day, as there is plenty of shade and the views are different because you are in the middle of the island.

There are no shops there now, since the one in the square closed but there is a kafenion or café bar which is open….sometimes… around 7.30pm. It stays open until the owner gets tired and wants to go to bed. It's pot luck. If you do visit in the daytime make sure you bring a drink and some food with you. The main church here is Agia Paraskevi and if you walk up to the graveyard you can see both sides of the island. The village festival takes place on 14th August for the population of around 350, in the summer months.

The villages of Kastellani mesi, Kouramades and Kokkini were lovely in their own way but when it came to choosing the final twenty to be included in the book unfortunately these three would not be added.

I enjoyed alternating my days of riding out to the villages and having a day off in between. It took the pressure off somehow and definitely gave me the chance to recharge my batteries. After racing around the villages everyday in May this pace suited me better. Although the pressure was still there on my days out having find out about the history of the villages a holiday every other day gave me time to relax and go over my notes and photographs.

My next day out would be a little further up the central region to the east and the boundary of the central area. I would head up and over the countryside from Temploni and this road would bring me to the main road at Gouvia. From there I would take the east coast road to Dassia and turn of left to Kato Korakiana and then to Ano Korakiana.

As you may remember, Kato Korakiana was the first place I had ever been to in 1987 and I had returned to many times over the years. This time I would see the village for what it truly was and not just a place to sleep with most of the time spent in Dassia and Ipsos.

Kato Korakiana.

Kato Korakiana is also known as Katomeri which means "lower place". 20 kilometres northeast from Corfu town, the village lies at a height of 100 metres above sea level and is near the tourist resorts of Dassia and Ipsos.

A big village with a population of around 950, its history goes back more than five hundred years and has attracted many famous poets and royalty. There are several churches here including saint Nicholas and saint Demetrius. The Turks invaded in 1537 (Barbarossa) and again in 1716. Besides the threat of the raids the whole region suffered land slides, some of which account for myths and legends. A geological phenomenon in the area, which was discovered before World

War II, is a tunnel (Grava tou Menigou). The locals will tell you that it leads to an underground river; which flows under the sea and into the coasts of Ambrakikos Bay, near Preveza on the Greek mainland.

This is where the 19th century Greek poet Gerasimos Markoras lived and worked, and nearby the house of the 20th century lyrical poet Lorentsos Mavillis. Here you will find the medieval Castello Mibelli villa of the Polylas family . The Castle has been visited by many famous people from Europe; among them, The Emperor of Austria Franz Josep, the Emperor of Germany Keiser Willelm, the king of Italy, Vittorio Emmanuelle, the kings of Greece, George I and George II (who settled permanently here from 1936 till 1939).

It was also here in 1844 that the Italian brothers Emilio and Attilio Bandiera planned an attempted rebellion in Southern Italy: unfortunately this didn't happen due to betrayal.

A short ride up the road bought me to Ano Korakiana. I call this village the "Village of the Churches". Like its sister village down the road I remember walking here from Kato Korakiana one day and looking around the village. We came to a flight of concrete steps with a dozen kittens jumping about and play fighting. They were a mixture of tortoishell, tabby, black and white of all ages and fathers most likely. We walked around the backstreets but didn't reach the main street so our memories of the village were very much that of ruins and overgrown gardens. How wrong we were. If we had ventured further we would have come away with a very different view.

Ano Korakiana.

Ano Korakiana is a historic settlement 19 kilometres north of Corfu town. The village was first inhabited during the medieval times and a lot of traditional aspects of that time have been maintained. Ano Korakiana was mainly populated by noble families, who still give a dynamic presence with the strong structure of the houses and the preserved characteristics of the 18th century.

Korakiana was almost destroyed in 1537 when it was invaded by the Turkish army Highredin Barbarossa. In 1716 it was attacked again but managed to survive due to the settlement of people from the Greek mainland. The village flourished economically during the English occupancy; where the majority of the local residents worked in trade, contributing to the cultural development of the region. The village was first populated as far back as 1204 with people from Asia and Thrace and then, in the Venetian age, by people from the Aegean, Peleponnese and Epirus.

Today, 900 people live permanently in Ano Korakiana. The terrain is rough with narrow paved streets, surrounded by emerald trees. There is a shop and a kafeneion but for some reason tavernas have struggled to survive here, even with the large amount of residents and the resorts nearby.

The village is known for the considerable number of churches, 37 in total, and the long tradition in folklore music and ceramic art. Ano Korakiana keeps a great balance among the rich spiritual life and the natural environment overlooking the island's eastern side filled with olive groves and fruit trees.

I needed to pick up a few things from Corfu town and on the way back I took the opportunity to go to Kompitsi. A winding road took me to the centre and I parked on the school yard opposite the main church. I took some photographs and talked to a young lady about the history of the village but this was not my main priority today. I wanted to know where the "Venetian well" was as it wasn't sign posted? The local girl spoke good English and pointed me in the right direction. I thanked her, turned the corner and found the steps that led down to the well. The path was overgrown and made from stones. After fifty metres was a dead end but a gaze to the left gave me a full frontal view of the well. I walked forward and stood before the magnificent façade. The walls were painted in a deep pink red with three arches boarded with a white outline. The centre arch was taller than the other two either side and this was where the water well opening was. On the left of me was a high pink wall which was the boundary to the great mansion house next door. To my right was a short pink wall where the villagers would have placed their buckets full of water. It has the appearance of a small church with its central apex and columns in the corners. The sad thing is the site looked neglected at the time somewhat but I have been back a few times since and can report that it has been painted in Corfu pink and is looking great.

Kompitsi.

Kompitsi lies 8 kilometres west of Corfu town on the road to Pelekas with the turning uphill on the left. A village of unique beauty, spread on the crest of a line of hills, with stunning vistas, it is surrounded by forests of chestnut trees and pines.

At the new cultural centre you can admire a unique collection of approximately 3000 automobile miniatures, while a little further up you can enjoy a cup of coffee at the village's traditional coffee house. The most contemporary part of the settlement, under the hillside and along the road to the town; has shops, restaurants, coffee houses and whatever you may need for your holiday.

On the hill of the village of Kompitsi, under a farmhouse of the Venetian period with a remarkable chimney, stands the Venetian fountain. It was built in a peculiar architectural baroque style, painted in a deep pink colour and is where the villagers used to get their water. The water supply is now taken from the three taps in the schoolyard, opposite the church of the apostles. This is where I stock up on our water when we visit Corfu.

As you go down the path to the fountain, a few meters from the square of the village, you pass in front of the former catholic convent. This has a column lined atrium and is now a private residence. The route to the fountain, with the stone paved path and the verdurous landscape all around, is truly fascinating.

Kompitsi has a population of around 600 and on 29th June the village celebrates saints Peter and Paul day with a festival in the square.

If I travel from Pelekas to Benitses or Messonghi I will take the central road east through the village of Gastouri. It is steeped in history and has some nice cafes and tavernas on the main street. In the lower part of the village there is the Sisi water well and some taps where the locals wash there clothes in the fresh waters from higher ground. Here is the largest Maple tree that I have ever found on Corfu. Its width must be ten feet across and its cover is immense.

Gastouri.

One of the most famous villages in Corfu is Gastouri because it is here that the Achilleion Palace is located. Built in 1890 for The Empress of Austria, Elisabeth of Bavaria, also known as Sisi, it is one of the most visited places on Corfu. After Elisabeth's death, the German Kaiser Wilhelm II bought it as a summer residence. Purists will say that the Palace is filled with modern replica statues - commissioned by Sisi in her fascination for Greek Culture - and that the architecture of the building is a poor attempt to imitate the great temples of the empire. Personally, I love it. The Palace is over 120 years old after all and the statues are now well weathered. The gardens are well tendered and lead to the magnificent 7 metre high bronze statue of Achilles. Inside on the staircase there is a huge painting of Achilles riding around Troy after defeating Hector in the Trojan War. The views from here overlook Kanoni and Corfu Airport to the east and you can watch the aeroplanes coming in to land.

The village is built on two levels: a lower part where there is a "well" given to the people by Sisi and an upper part, where the Palace lies. 10km south of Corfu Town, close the resort of Benitses, the way up from the coast road is full of S bends, but when you reach the village you are greeted with some spectacular old mansions and pretty coloured houses. The village festival (panigiri) is held on the 23rd August in the square (platea) which is behind the road, is transformed by the 950 residents who turn out for the celebrations. The Churches here are Aghios Markianos and Aghios Nicolaos and like so many villages on Corfu well worth a visit as they imposing from the outside and extremely impressive on the inside.

The lower part of the village has a famous Bakery where the bread is traditionally baked in an old stone oven. People travel long distances to get their daily bread here because of the Bakers reputation.

That would be it for this holiday as the family had now arrived to spend the second week with me and I had agreed to spend some quality time with them and take a rest.

Before I knew it, the final and last visit to Corfu of the year had arrived and I still had a few villages to go to. It was now October and I was to incorporate the holiday with a few days on the road, a few days rest and a birthday party for me in Pelekas.

My plan this time was to head to the south of the central region and visit the mountain villages of Pendati and Agioi

Deka. I could then finish the book with my own village of Pelekas to finish the first book in style.

You can see Pendati jutting out on the headland south from Pelekas with the lights sparkling in the distance above the sea when the sun goes down. But the roads that lead to the village on the hill are narrow and very steep. The views from here are spectacular as you look back north to Agios Gordios, Pelekas and beyond. There is a great taverna half way up to the church which lies at the top of the village.

Pendati.

If you are on holiday in the resort of Agios Gordios, there are a cluster of small villages just a few kilometres walk away. Kato Garouna, Ano Pavliana, Kato

Pavliana and Pendati are all within reach of Agios Gordios but there are some very steep climbs here. The reward though is well worth it. There are fantastic views over the bay and the famous Ortholithi rock.

If you follow the road that leads to Ano Garouna village, you can wander through the picturesque narrow paths of the village. Follow the uphill road which starts from the village square and it will lead you up to Panteleimonas mountain. It is here that you can see Agios Gordios down below and from the other side, the town of Corfu.

 Carry on up to the Panteleimonas mountain, where there is the starting point for the Corfu parascending club. Watch them as they run and leap off the edge of the mountain to catch the thermals. These keep them in the air for what seems ages before they land smoothly on Agios Gordios beach - hopefully missing the crowds of sunbathers.

Pendati is worth visiting for the interesting church of Panaghia Odigitria (The Holy Virgin, The Leader) dating from the 19th century. It also has a marvellous view of the Ionian Sea.

The local festival, or panigiri, takes place on the 26th of October. It is held in honour of Aghios Dimitrios and many people attend from the villages nearby.

The final day out was to the village of Agioi Deka in the south of the central region. It lies on Corfu's spine at the boundary of the border to the south. When I arrived at the main street I parked the scooter and looked around for a place where I could have frape and see if I could talk to some locals. On the corner of the street was a very dangerous bend and this was the place I headed for as it looked like a café/kafenion. As I approached I was immediately in the direct vision of half a dozen Greek men with ages ranging from about thirty to seventy. They were shouting and laughing before I made my way over but all went quiet as I walked in and said "Kalimera sas" (Good morning") to people you don't know. A muffled kalimera came back and I sat down close buy and ordered a cold coffee in Greek. When my frape arrived I asked the lads where the Pantokrator mountain was again in Greek but they wanted to know where I was from. I said I was from England but I owned a place in Pelekas. The next thing I knew was that anyone who spoke English was asking me questions about Pelekas. Some of them knew the village and told me some stories from years ago which was nice. They then told me a little about their village and how to get to the Pantokrator church at the top of the mountain. I thanked them and rode down the road to the entrance to the "All Mighty" track. At the foot of the concrete road was the smallest religious building I had ever seen. It was no bigger than one metre wide by two metres in length. The front door was half wood at the bottom and half glass at the top. The top had a Christian cross inscribed from top to bottom on it and there was a blue and white Greek flag on one side and the yellow and black Greek Orthodox flag on the other. It was surrounded by a criss-cross pattern in newly painted white and was also on the entrance to a large house so maybe it was a gift from the family for their good fortune?

At the top of the mountain is a monastery and a chapel. When I was taking photographs an EasyJet plane passed by below where I was standing. Now that was strange.

Agioi Deka.

Agioi Deka village nestles on a hill some 250 meters up on the side of the second largest mountain in Corfu, standing at 576 meters above sea level.

Agioi Deka means "Ten Saints" in Greek and the story goes that 50 Christian

Saints were being persecuted in Albania. Ten escaped to Corfu and set up a Monastery on top of the mountain. The forty who were left behind were martyred hence the name of the port in Albania (opposite Kassiopi) which is called Aghi Seranda (The Forty Saints). It is a quiet village and can be found 15 kilometres south of Corfu Town taking the main road to Sinarades. Population is around 350 and the views from the village itself are great.

The road up to the top of the mountain is a right hand turn some 3km through the village. Take the sign for Pantokrator. The accent from the village is a steep one but well worth the climb when you reach the summit. If you don't fancy the walk - and it is a long steep climb - it is possible to ride a scooter or drive a car up. At the top is the huge white "Golf Ball" you can see from all over Corfu. This is an air navigation system. There is also a small Chapel and the Monastery of Pantokrator. The views from here looking to the east and west coasts are breath taking.

Walk or drive back down to the Village for a well earned drink and take in the slow pace of traditional Greek life. There are a couple of tavernas here and a Kafenion on the corner. This is a great place to sit as the cars that come around the sharp corner often have to reverse back to make way for the traffic coming down the main street.

I don't need to describe Pelekas to you now as I'm sure you know enough about it already. But, it was a fitting way to finish the last holiday of the year in the comfort zone of my own village. I couldn't wait to get back to the UK to finish the first eBook and to release it to the media. But here is the history of Pelekas.

Pelekas.

Pelekas lies on the west coast of Corfu, 15 kilometres west of Corfu town and the airport. It can be found in the historical archives of Corfu as far back as the 16th century and in church records, dating from the 17th century. The origin of the village's name is not known. One suggestion is that it derives from the word "pelekis"; which was a type of ancient axe, used by the villagers for cutting wood or stone. In the lower part of the village is the

Theotokos Odigitria church, where the service takes place for the yearly panigiri or festival on 23rd August. This swells the local population from around 500 to over 1,000, in the main plateia or Square. In the upper part of the village is the Saint Nikolaos church. A fifteen minute walk uphill will bring you to the Kaisers Throne viewpoint and a third church called Thetokos Evangelistria. All these churches date from around 1750.

There are many tavernas and café bars in Pelekas which is unusual for a inland village. This is a legacy from the late 70's and 80's; when many Scandinavians and Europeans took advantage of cheap student bus and railway tickets, to visit Corfu. Pelekas beach, known locally as Kontogialos, became the backpackers' daytime paradise and the village (a twenty minute walk uphill) became the centre for their nightlife. The Pelekas Cultural Society promotes cultural awareness, maintains local traditions and organises festivals, as well as running choirs and dance groups. There is also a costume museum on the main road up to the village. This houses a private collection of traditional Greek dress dating from the 19th century.

So, next time you are in Corfu; take a trip to Kaisers Throne, have some lunch in the village square and then head down to the beach for a well deserved swim. Sunbathe on the sandy beach and watch the dramatic sunset over the sea.

The first thing I did when I got back to England was to get in touch with my Internet man Leon, and the eBook designer, Jay. As soon as the design was ready, Leon would upload it onto the website and it would be for sale. Jay did a nice design with exactly the format I wanted showing the history of the villages and six snapshot photographs underneath like the old polaroid cameras used to take. My job was to upload it on to the Amazon eBook format so then we would have two platforms to sell it on. It was ready to launch at the end of October and I advertised it on the Corfu Facebook groups and pages. We had a great response from the members and by April 2013 I had raised over 500 euros for the Corfu charities. Not a bad return when you think that the eBook was priced at £3.99. Most eBooks at the time were priced at 99p but I thought to myself, what is the point of charging 99p for a book that has taken me three holidays to write and has taken me over 1,000 kilometres to the most remote villages to research. Surely the members will respond to my call to help the poorest people at this crucial time of poverty on Corfu. Yes was the answer to my question and I thank you all from the bottom of my heart to this day as in the next editions proved to be a catalyst to the many good things that happened, in my humble opinion, to the awakening of what the less fortunate on Corfu were experiencing. You and I were having a great holiday on our favourite Island but the reality was that the people in general were struggling to make ends meet.

When I started out on my original quest I was unaware of the charity work that was taking place on Corfu. I knew that the Agni website was helping to feed and neuter cats. There were a couple of places that were dealing with the dogs and the Donkey sanctuary was looking after the poor and abandoned donkey's. I had no idea what work was going on to help the poorer people of Corfu until I found out about the soup kitchens and the donations of food from customers and supermarkets. I had a vision to make the cause more well known on Corfu and through the social media more well known around Europe and the World.

Let me take this opportunity to say that the Greek people are a very proud nation. Charity to them is very personal and is mainly dealt with amongst themselves and after many discussions with my friends in the village I got the message of "Bravo file mou" (Well done my friend) but proceed with humility, compassion and caution. With this in mind I contacted the Red Cross charity in Corfu town. I spoke to a lovely lady called Emily and she said that it would be great if I could donate food and supplies when I came to Corfu the following spring.

So, I had achieved my first goal. I had an eBook on the central region that was selling well. I had some money to spend and I had a plan to write the second eBook about the north of Corfu the following year to keep the donations coming in for the poorer families for next year. I was feeling pretty pleased at this time and used to look everyday on the website to see how many people had bought the book. For a working class kid like me this was an amazing experience at the time as I felt that I was on the verge of helping poor families on Corfu and actually making a difference to peoples lives. The following year would give me highs and lows but I was ready for the challenge.

5. Part 2. Corfu North.

I couldn't wait to get out to Corfu in the spring of 2013. I had money to give to the poor families and I had a second eBook to write about the North of the Island. How could it get any better than this? But, this second year would prove to be the biggest challenge of all and it would test my commitment to the cause to the absolute limit.

I flew to Corfu on a Friday night and after cleaning the apartment on Saturday I planned my first day out on the following day. On this holiday I would go north and I would also be in Pelekas for the Greek Easter. First on my list was the village of Krini in the north west and the Angelokastro castle. I stopped in the square and talked to two old ladies who were sitting on the circular wall under the cover of a tree in the shade. Helena and Ilene were in their 80's and were both dressed from head to toe in black even down to their pop socks which came up to their knees. They both had silver hair and giggled like little girls as I approached and greeted them in Greek. They told me about some of the history with the help of hand gestures and pointed me in the direction of the church. They were very sweet and posed generously for me when I asked if I could take a photograph of them. Of the thousands of photographs I have taken on my thirty years of visiting Corfu, this remains one of my favourite's.

Krini.

Krini, the true gateway to the Angelokastro medieval castle, is just a few kilometres northwest of Paleokastritsa. As you follow the road to the sea, the castle view suddenly appears from nowhere in all its magnificent grandeur, standing before you like a giant crowned head of Zeus. This is a small but very picturesque village, well kept and nicely painted, built on the slopes of Istoni mountain, which has some 266 residents. The story goes that Krini has existed since Homer's time, but evidence suggests that the villagers' surnames refer to officials of the medieval Byzantine army. They are the descendants of the "Akrites", the guards of the borders of the Byzantine empire.

The village square is crowned by a single tree, circled with a stone sitting area, that stakes its claim as the centre of the plateia (square), where the men gather to talk and drink coffee. There is a kafeneio and the church of Agios Nikolaos which has some marble archangel pictures. A one kilometre walk downhill will bring you to the the Palioklisies region and the start of the ascent to the Angelokastro castle, "Castle of Angels". At a height of 305 metres to the Acropolis, the castle was one of the most important fortifications in Byzantine times as it was the lookout point for the protection of the northwest coastline.

Two early Christian slabs were unearthed in 1997, suggesting that the area was occupied in early Byzantine times, between the 5th and 7th centuries. The castle dates from around the 11th or 12th century and was virtually impregnable. It withstood the attacks from the Turks in 1571 and 1716 when much of Corfu was sacked. The views from the castle are outstanding and from here you can see the Diapontian islands. There is a church dedicated to the Archangel

Michael, a tiny chapel dedicated to Saint Kyriaki, a cemetery and a circular tower. I for one will be visiting again.

From Krini I rode up through Makrades to the twin villages of Prinilas and Pagi. As I turned the bend to enter Makrades an old man jumped out from nowhere and nearly knocked me off my bike. I stopped for a minute to see why he had flagged me down and saw that he was selling home made wine. On this occasion I declined and thanked him and went on my way but, I would return to see him in the future many times.

Makrades.

When referring to the village of Makrades, one guide book describes it as "a curious tradition of roadside stalls whose energetic owners could probably sell refrigerators to Eskimos." A bit harsh in my opinion, but, I have indeed been waved down by owners of the many shops selling homemade wine and handmade products. When confronted with a sample of wine and a big smile, it's hard to resist the charms of the people from this village.

It is a very unusual village by Greek standards and in some ways quite European in its layout. It has the rare mixture of the old village with a high street of shops. I presume that the reason for this was the desire of the local population to take advantage of the emerging tourist trade created from the visitors to the Angelokastro Castle.

The village is best reached from the resort of Paleokastritsa. Turn left up the winding road to Lakones and drive a few kilometres further on to reach the village. After a couple of kilometres, a wide main street greets you with tourist shops either side selling every Corfu gift you can think of. The odd taverna and kafeneion is sprinkled in between to keep you fed and watered as you buy all the presents for the family back home.

But that is not all Makrades has to offer. Take the road behind the street on the bend and you will see the old village, with narrow streets only wide enough for a donkey to pass through. The church of Saint Paraskevi is here and the feast day for the 240 residents falls on 26th July. Saint Paraskevi was a Christian martyr from the 2nd century who was born in Rome in around

140AD to Greek parents. The word Paraskevi means Friday in Greek and that is the day that she was born.

Prinilas & Pagi.

I have friends who live in Prinilas and visited them recently. Mandy and Terry Lockett bought an old property on the edge of the village and rebuilt and extended it from scratch. There is a small church opposite the house and the view from the front is hill full of different trees of scores of every shade of green you could think of. Sprinkled on the lower foothills of the hill are several purple Jasmine trees. When we met up with them they took us to the nearby village of Pagi to meet the famous Jimmy (Dimitris) from the 007 James Bond café bar. The square that the café stands in is awash with flower pots and bougainvillea dressing the taverna opposite and the house next door.

Prinilas village has a panoramic view over the bay of Agios Georgios and the sunsets here are legendary. There is a taverna where you can gaze at the sheer cliffs as they descend down to the small beach and the sea. The village has a small kafeneion.

The most common surname in the village is Gialopsos possibly deriving from the ancient Greek expression "aigialon opsontes" meaning "they will see the sea".

Prinilas constituted the administrative centre of the Byzantine domination in the 11th century. The past prosperity can be seen with the impressive mansions of the 20th century, that are scattered around the village. Take a walk in the traditional alleyways and visit the chapel of Agios Nikolaos which dates back to the 14th century.

Pagi has a unique history too. When the Cretan village of Chandakas was occupied by the Turks in the 17th century, its residents moved to the Corfiot village of nearby Pagi or Pagoi. The area had been settled since Roman times, according to the findings of the National Archaeological Service. There are relics of the Georgantas mansion, which dates back to the Venetian period when Pagi was an administration centre, and also the Synadinos mansion with its military emblems.

The villages are close together and both worth a visit in their own right because, although they are small, the history is tangible in the very walls of the houses and mansions.

I had started out early in the morning and it was a good job because I still had to go further north to Afionas and up to Arillas where I was to spend the night with Alex Christou and his family. Alex is a pioneer in the alternative travel business and promotes a "Green future" of tourism in Arillas.

Afionas is probably the most photographed village of them all on Corfu. With its blue and white coloured houses and abundant flowers it is a very pretty village. From here you can look down onto the beautiful crescent shaped sandy bay of Agios Georgios and a half an hour walk down to the sea will bring you to the extraordinary twin bay of Porto Timoni.

Afionas.

Situated at the northern end of Agios Georgios bay; Afionas offers a magnificent view of the whole bay and surrounding hills right across to the distant cliffs of Akri Falakra, the headland behind Paleokastritsa. The village is 300 metres above sea level and has around 300 residents. In ancient times there were sentries there, to monitor invaders and warn the people at Angelokastro by lighting beacons. The views along the north west coast of Corfu are quite breathtaking, and to the west you can see the small islands of Gravia, Sikia and Gineka. From the village, a path winds across headland and down to Porto Timoni where there is reputedly the ruins of a fortress, built in 300 BC by Pirros, King of Epirus.

Afionas village is known to have been first inhabited during the 6th century BC. It was supposedly abandoned a little later and then re-inhabited during the 6th century AD by Avars, a tribe from Central Asia. On the northwest side of Akri Arilla (Point Arilla) there are excavations which have uncovered a village dating back to the Neolithic times. There is a story of the traditional Greek stone column, situated on a small hill behind Dionysos taverna, being destroyed by a bomb from a German plane during World War 2. There is a small, red and white painted torpedo on display in the centre of the village, on a wall adjacent to the church, with an olive wood shop opposite. All of the buildings in the square have been recently painted in traditional Corfu colours of deep pink, terracotta and yellow. However, as you walk up the winding streets of the village, the colours change to mostly blue and white and the houses take on the appearance of those commonly found in the Cyclades. Afionas is known locally as the green village or garden village, as there are so many flowers that adorn the houses there. The main event of the year is the festival dedicated to the church of Saint John on the 24th of June.

The minor roads of the northwest are narrow but in good condition and asphalted. The views were spectacular.

The Diapontian Islands, off the northern coast of Corfu; the unspoilt sandy beaches, as golden now as they were when the Phaeacians sailed the waters there; hilltop villages with varying architecture the further north you go; the amazing sunsets, often diverse due to April's changing weather and of course the flowers and shrubs awaking from their winter sleep.

I was getting a little tired now as I had been on the road all day and as I entered Arillas the sun became less fierce. I had arranged to meet Alex in a taverna on the front and as I arrived early I ordered a much welcomed large Mythos. Alex arrived and took me to his house where I had a cat nap before settling down with the family for a dinner of pastisada and some delicious home made wine. We exchanged all night of how we could promote Corfu for the generations to come and he thanked me for the work I was doing as a Xenos (Stranger).

The next morning he made me a breakfast of boiled eggs and coffee and wished me on my way. It was the first time I had eaten with a Greek family in their house, as apposed to a holiday home or a closed taverna and it was a special experience.

I passed through Kanadades and Magoulades on the way to Avliotes and would later learn about the Children's home there that was supported entirely on donations. I viewed the sandy beach of Agios Stefanos from the hill road above but this was not a day for sunbathing or swimming for me as I had work to do.

Avliotes.

Avliotes is a mountainous settlement lying on the northwest side of the island, 40 kilometres from Corfu town. It is a pretty, well kept village set against a background of hills. There are a few nicely painted shops and a kafeneion to serve the population of around 900. The village has an abundance of attractive and traditional architecture, but its most impressive building is the eighteenth century church of Iperagias Theotokou Odigitrias, which stands proudly on a huge platform at the top of the village. Although often locked, you can still admire the solid structure and its two belfries; one attached to the church and a smaller one free standing, beside the church. There is also a small cemetery in the corner of the church grounds.

The villages in the northwest were built on sandstone ridges to the highest point, which gives the area the sandy beaches below. They were built high and close together as space was at a premium, to avoid the cold, damp line below. This explains why the families of the village have plots of land below and sometimes of some distance away.

A good time to visit is on Clean Monday before Easter, as the village holds a traditional Carnival. Adults and children alike dress up and parade the streets on floats, before joining in with the festivities. If you're in need of something to eat, there is a basic taverna halfway along the main street. Here, cheap and tasty grills can be enjoyed on the vine covered terrace whilst admiring the tremendous views inland. Bear in mind that Avliotes is at the end of the Sidari bus route from Corfu Town, so it is only accessible by public transport via the north coast. It is, however, little more than a pleasant half an hour walk from either Agios Stefanos or Sidari or a short taxi ride away.

I was now in the village that is the most northwest settlement on Corfu. It lies in the very top left corner of the Island and is remote but easily accessed fro Sidari. The taverna at the top of the steep cliff is famous here and a newly built walkway made from glass juts out from the edge of the cliff to give visitors a viewing point and a photograph opportunity as the sunsets here are spectacular.

Peroulades.

Peroulades is a beautiful, old Greek village located in the northwest of Corfu about 40 kilometres from Corfu town and is currently under preservation for its cultural and architectural heritage from Venetian times.

The village is set high above the sea, at the top of steep cliffs that drop down to a small beach. It is well known for its spectacular sunsets. It is so far north that it has been called by some, "the village that time forgot".

There are a few tavernas here in the square mainly filled with walkers and sightseers travelling through. The population is of around 800 and the church is devoted to Saint Nicholas. Some of the houses are deserted now but as the crisis in Athens deepens, locals in the villages all over Corfu expect family members to return to their places of birth and once again fill the streets as they did generations ago.

Although the main income here is from the olive groves, many of the people work in the surrounding tourist areas, the main one being Sidari.

Many people who have repeat holidays in Sidari have a soft spot for Peroulades and return each year to eat in their favourite taverna or kafeneion as they have become friends with the local people. Only a few kilometres from Sidari are some great places to visit.

There is the Canal D'Amour with its weathered rock formations and small coves. Loggas Beach for its famous sunsets and Cape Drastis where the rocks dramatically protrude into the sea.

I had a two hour journey ahead of me on the scooter to get back to Pelekas but I couldn't resist riding that extra mile to sea the Sunset beach and Cape Drastis. I was so far north now I thought I would have a nose bleed decided to head back to Pelekas armed with some more villages for the next eBook. As I rode back I thought about all the lovely villages I had been to and thought to myself how big Corfu was. It was then I named the Island " The little big Island" I had a dilemma. Do I continue to use the scooter to travel around the villages? I was well placed in Pelekas in the central part of the Island and so going north and south I had the least amount of miles to travel. I knew the distances but the roads were often not much more than tracks. If I had a car it would be much easier but then I wouldn't be able to stop in an instance to take a photograph and parking in the villages was a problem due to space. No contest, although the scooter was more tiring I loved the freedom of the open road and I must admit that when I ventured off the main road I would take my helmet off. I would take off my jeans and trainers and swap them for a pair of shorts and a pair of sandals. Pame tora! (Let's go now!)

The following day I had been invited to a coffee morning at the Anglican Holy

Trinity church in Corfu town. I was to give a presentation about the first eBook so I printed off the pages and placed them in a folder for everyone to see. I also had a pdf disc of the eBook made so they could buy it and simply play it on their laptop or computer and to save them downloading it. I took twenty pdf's with me and sold every one for five euros. Bob and Tricia came down from Loutses to show their support and we went for lunch later at Nino's in town.

I decided to take a break now and enjoy what time I had left with my friends in Pelekas for the Easter celebrations. It had been a good visit and I was pleased with what I had done.

It was June when I returned to Corfu arriving on the late night Friday flight from Manchester. On Sunday morning I set of on the scooter with my battered old map, a cold bottle of water and enough tobacco to last me a few days just in case I got lost. I was heading into unknown territory and who knows what lay before me in the mountainous north. This trip would be to the heart of the central north, the untouched villages, the places that time forgot.

The first village I came to was Skripero where I was surprised to encounter a set of traffic lights. They lights were on red but I couldn't see any traffic and the road was quite wide so I just carried on. It wasn't until I got half way down the narrowing road that I saw a huge lorry coming towards me. No problem, there was enough room for both of us.

Skripero.

Traffic on the main artery northwest often slows to a near halt, as it snakes through the narrow main street of Skripero. Traffic lights through the village though, have brought a sense of order to this busy gateway to the north. Skripero is a large village located 18 kilometres northwest of Corfu town with rich history and culture, mostly known for its philharmonic society that was founded in 1909 and is still active. Skripero also has old Venetian mansions and an excellent folklore tradition. It is the administrative centre for much of central northern Corfu and has a population of around 600. There is a shop, a kafeneion and a taverna all located on the busy main road. The pace of life however is a typically slow one, as the locals simply ignore the passing traffic and continue with their everyday lives. There are the churches of Saint Stephen and Yperageia Theotokos Liviotissa and the monastery of Yperageia Theotokos Vlachernon.

Most people pass through the Skripero and remain unaware of what the village has to offer. I found it was a good place to stop for a rest because of its central location to all central and northern resorts. Park your car and head for the taverna or kafeneion and sit and watch the traffic pass by as you enjoy your break. Look opposite and you will see the green canvas backdrop of Mount Tsouka rising above to 620 metres and creating a frame for the main church elevated in front of you. Order your food or drinks and whilst you are waiting, wander up past the church where there is a maze of tracks with more tumbling down old houses than occupied ones.

About 3 kilometres further northwest, at the top of the ridge, Troumbeta is an important junction, with shortcuts to Paleokastritsa and Agios Georgios (NW) bearing west on either side of the village, while the main road veers towards the north coast and resorts of Sidari, Acharavi and Kassiopi.

From Skripero the winding road took me up higher and higher through the villages of Agros and Agrafi to my destination and my breakfast to the large village of Karousades. I parked up and bought a couple of bananas from the mini market then sat down to take in the midday sun. After spending over an hour walking around and taking photographs I decided to head home as I had six friends arriving the following day and I needed to change my hat and put my tour rep badge on.

Karousades.

In the north western part of the island and 40 kilometres from Corfu town is the village of Karousades. The village has approximately 1300 inhabitants and was established in 20BC by the Karousses, refugees from the Pontian region of the Black Sea. During the Byzantine period, it was a command post with a well developed economy. In 1453, the Theotokis family settled in the village, establishing a great dynasty which went on to play a leading role in the economic and political life of the island. Their grand mansion, built in 1500, is preserved today. It is built in a beautiful location and is worth visiting; just to walk through the paths of the village which, by Corfu standards, is quite large. There are several churches here, two of which are devoted to Saint George and Saint Nicholas. The village festival takes place on the 26th September in honour of Saint James Theologian.

Today it is a popular village with bars, tavernas, shops, supermarkets, a school and Police station and does not have to rely on tourists to survive; although they are of course welcome. There are several beaches that are within walking distance of the village, such as Gualos, Andreas, Astrakeri and Agnos beach for those who want to sunbathe off the beaten track. As I left the village I noticed what looked like a newly renovated coffee bar called Kalamaki, which means "Straw" in Greek. Unfortunately it was closed, as I could have used a well earned frappe with water before heading back home. The vertical backboards to the hanging orange lights, the hand carved stools, the narrow shelves standing on the forked trunk were all made from olive wood, as was the narrow floor....Beautiful.

Only a few kilometres from the resorts of Sidari and Roda, this village is well worth a visit. I will return when the café is open!

When my guests arrived I had arranged for four of them to stay at Alexandros taverna rooms in the village and two of them would stay with me. We met at Alexandros for an English breakfast which contained bacon, eggs and fresh tomato with tea and toast. I asked Alex if his mother could fry the tomato in a pan but he said no, it will make to much mess. We then walked the fifteen minute road uphill to the Kaisers throne viewpoint. The lads were impressed with the views and we walked over the road to the Levant hotel as they have a nice swimming pool there. Lunch was served by the owner Dandis down by the pool and he didn't complain once about the fact that he had to walk up and down several steps with all the food and drinks. We did ask if he wanted any help but he declined and gave us a wry smile.

The next day two of my friends who were staying with me asked me how I was getting on with the second book and I said it was going well but the distances I was having to cover on the scooter were long and tiring. I told them I still had to visit Kassiopi in the top northeast corner of the Island yet so they suggested we hired a car for a couple of days to give me a break from the scooter. We took the Temploni road to Gouvia and drove through the flat resort roads of Dassia and Ipsos and headed north on the east coast road. We past the resorts of Barbati, Nissaki and Kalami and arrived in Kassiopi where we struggled to park. We walked around the village and scrambled up to the newly renovated castle that overlooks the harbour. I was surprised to find the track up to the castle was uneven with loose stones considering so much money had been spent on the castle itself.

Kassiopi.

Kassiopi is a village located in the northeast region of Corfu, whose history dates back over 2200 years to before Christ. There are two different stories as to who were the first inhabitants of Kassiopi. One is that the first inhabitants were from a village of the same name from the mainland, who came to Kassiopi during the years 227-160BC They came across because living conditions there were made difficult by barbaric invasions. The second view is that the King of Epirus, with the intention of creating a strategic shelter, decided to increase the population of Corfu and so he conquered in 281BC and transfered inhabitants from the mainland. Kassiopi became an important hideaway and significant port. Neronas, the King of Rome, stayed there and set up the baths in Kassiopi. It had a workshop that made its own currency, a sure sign of power in the region. The first inhabitants of Kassiopi worshiped the ancient Greek god Cassio Dia and built a temple in his honour, which was one of the most beautiful temples of its time. The church on the main road to the harbour is built upon its ruins and is called Yperageia Theotokos Kassopitra. Kassiopi was destroyed by the Venetians during the Roman Empire and completely deserted by the Turkish during the invasion of 1537. In 1604, priests from Epirus established themselves in Kassiopi so as to once again turn it into a powerful state.

Although a major resort on the island, few people wander up to the old village where the castle dates back to Byzantine times lies. The fortress was used as a fortification and lookout post against invaders and is currently being renovated to its former glory. With a census population of over 1,000 it would be difficult to estimate the true village number as the boundaries have been blurred by tourism. Look around the castle area, whose access is opposite the main church, and you will find the old village houses behind the newer buildings.

I then drove them to the village of Old Peritheia. It was the first time I had been to this village so it was nice to walk around with Bob and Dave and discover the eerie broken down buildings for the first time together.

Old Peritheia.

The village was established during Byzantine times, when pirate raids forced people to abandon fertile coastal plains for more inaccessible regions. For many years Peritheia was a completely deserted village, but a few years ago two tavernas opened in the old square and gained a reputation for good food. Now there are five and a few of the old houses have been bought and restored into a four star motel. The owner of the "O Foros" taverna, Thomas, told me that there is an old couple of around 75 years of age that have lived there all of their lives. His taverna is open every day from the start of May until the end of October and then on weekends thereafter. The food was good and prices were very reasonable.

The historic village of Old Peritheia is situated in the northeast of the island and is about 35 kilometres from Corfu town. The best way to get there is to take the turn for Loutses from the resorts of Acharavi or Kassiopi. The road is narrow and winding towards the end, so drive with care! It is said to be the oldest permanently inhabited settlement in Corfu, dating back some 600 years and sits in a hollow on Corfu's highest mountain, Mount Pantokrator which stands at 906 metres. The mountain stands over the village like a guardian angel protecting it from the outside world. At one time the village was occupied by over 1500 people but lost all its inhabitants, due to population exchanges over the last century. There are only 130 stone houses, built entirely by hand, some of which have now fallen into ruins. The village with its cobbled streets and ancient houses is encircled by eight churches and set amidst beautiful countryside and bare hills. It is very strange to walk through the village, with its empty houses and dilapidated roofs, to think that there was once a thriving community living there. A visit here will give you memories you will never forget. Distinctive and picturesque, Old Peritheia is designated as an area of outstanding natural beauty and is a protected heritage site.

After a splendid lunch we drove down the narrow road from the village with some trepidation. Every bend seemed to offer us a sheer drop and Bob especially was a little concerned. Normality was resumed as we arrived at the junction of New Pertheia and we drove through Acharavi and Roda before taking the road south to Pelekas.

The next day we all went to Glyfada beach for the day and in the late afternoon we had to be at Agnes taverna in Pelekas as a friend of mine was coming down from Acharavi to interview me on camera about the book. Kevin Baker would do the interview and his friend Alan Smith would film the video. We talked about the idea about the book and what I wanted to achieve. My main aim was to get tourists to visit the wonderful villages and spend some tourist money there but also to raise money for the poorer families, children and animals on Corfu in this very difficult time. The interview went well and a month later Kevin launched it on YouTube. When I watched the video I thought how professional Kevin was but at the same time I felt very humble to be in the position I was in and it made me even more determined to reach my goal.

Thursday was a lazy day at Mirtiotissa beach and we took a timeout as we had a very busy day ahead of us the next day.

On Friday Bob Giles had driven all the way down from the hilltop village of Loutses in the north to meet us at the Lidl supermarket near the airport. The plan was to buy as much food as we could fit into his car as we could and take it to the Red cross in Corfu town. It was strange buying food in bulk. After a consultation by email with Emily who runs the Red cross we decided to buy two dozen of everything that she had suggested to us. They would need unperishable foods that would last so we bought rice, pasta, cooking oil, olive oil, vinegar, tins of tomatoes, biscuits, long life milk and sugar etc. Also, bathroom and kitchen items like, toilet roll, toothpaste, soap, bleach and more. When we arrived at the Red cross we were warmly greeted by Emily and her team of helpers. She told us that the food and supplies we had bought would be shared out and would feed up to thirty families and would be distributed immediately.

Then it was back to Pelekas for a change of clothes as I had arranged a charity football game with the local boys from the village to raise some more money and to sell the last few Corfu villages CD's. It was 6.00pm in the evening when we kicked off the match but it was still hot. Kevin and Alan had come down from Acharavi again to watch the match and we did another interview to complete the video. We revised the length of the match to fifteen minutes each way as the temperature was still at 30c. There were only a couple of Greek lads so we decided to mix the sides together to make it fair. The sides were made up of locals, Dutch and English. The match was level at 2 - 2 in the second half when I took a free kick from twenty yards out and it flew into the top right hand corner of the net. Ronaldo would have been proud of shot and it should have been the winning goal. But, my brother in law, Kenny who was playing in goal for them said he wasn't ready! OK I said as it was only a charity game. A minute later there was a 50/50 tackle and we had burst the ball. Game over, time for a well deserved beer.

My friends had gone back to the UK and I had a few days to myself. I reflected on the week that had passed and it seemed like a crazy dream. I had one spare day left so I filled up the scooter with petrol and off I went up to the northern villages of Spartilas and Strinilas. The views from these two villages are simply stunning and if writing a book was classed as work then I would do this for a living.

Spartilas.

The village of Spartilas nestles at a height of 400 metres and sits under the looming peak of Mount Pantokrator. Despite being only 23 kilometres north of Corfu town, the winding road uphill will make the journey seem much longer. Like many of Corfu's settlements, Spartilas lies at the "olive line" the contour above which the tree will not grow. Such a location meant that the inhabitants, in past days reliant on their crops and animals, would not have far to walk to their daily toil; downwards to their olive groves and up to their pastures. As villagers used to rely on donkeys for transport, the alleys which wind between the houses are narrow and just wide enough for a donkey and its panniers.

The old kafeneion is a place where the men still gather to discuss politics, while sipping Greek coffee and ouzo with water. Everywhere you look, architectural features catch the eye. Sandstone arches that lead to a storeroom under a 'bodzo', a first floor balcony which gives access to the living quarters. Stucco is painted on the walls, with multiple layers of colour, peeling and faded. Traditionally walls were lime washed, a practice still followed today by those wishing to preserve the integrity of older buildings. There are staircases of old marble and arched gateways that lead into overgrown gardens. Spartilas has been called the window of Corfu. With views that look south to the crescent shaped bay of Ipsos, Dassia, Gouvia and Kontokoli and to Corfu town. On a clear day, Paxos and Lefkada can also be seen in the distance. Being set between the mountain and the sea and oriented south, Spartilas enjoys a mild climate, neither too hot nor too cold.

The population of around 575 have two main Orthodox churches that are those of Saint Prophet Elijah and Saint Spyridon. There are a couple of tavernas with great views, and some wonderful old buildings which are slowly but elegantly decaying in dispersed amongst the occupied ones.

Strinilas.

Strinilas is the gateway to the Pantokrator summit. The village opens up a whole new world of discovery, going back in time to the fascinating rural life of Greece. The cool mountain air of Strinilas is refreshing as it is perched near the top of the highest mountain of Corfu, Mount Pantokrator. Visitors will also find that the architectural features of Strinilas are distinctly different from those found elsewhere on the island of Corfu. The village is conspicuous due to its highly resistant stones that can be found in abundance here and in other neighbouring areas. These hard stones are referred to as the 'strinaria' which is derived from the ancient Greek word "strinis", which literally means "hard".

No visit to the Strinilas village is ever complete without sampling the locally produced wine, Moschato; which has carved a niche for itself in the world of high quality wines. There are numerous elegant mountain tavernas where Moschato wine can be sampled. A remarkable feature of this wine is the distinct fragrance, which has endeared itself to many of its loyal customers worldwide. The mountainous road from Spartilas snakes its way to Strinilas and on this route are a few vantage points from which you can see a huge amount of the Corfu landscape. As you enter the village there is a nice square with a kafeneion on the left and a taverna on the right. There is plenty of parking and many people will stop here before making the final short journey to the

Pantokrator. The taverna here has the biggest Elm tree I have ever seen in Greece and gives a welcome shade as it covers all of the tables and beyond. There are two churches here. One is 50 metres north, past the square, up a small road and a turn to the right. The second one is signposted 100 metres before the village but be careful here as it is a dirt track with potholes and loose stones.

My third visit to Corfu was a ten day holiday with the family and I had a further five days on my own to do what I needed to complete part two of the book. This holiday would be a mixture of family days with visits to the northern villages and meetings with some special people who live on Corfu. To finish the second eBook I needed to go to Agios Markos, Kiprianades, Klimatia, Loutses, Nimfes and Sokraki. It would take two full days out to cover these villages so I decided to wait until the family had gone home before I started my final trips to the north.

Apart from Loutses which is on the Pantokratora mountain the other villages lay in the very heart of Corfu and nestle on the higher slopes of the Troumpeta mountain range. They are sleepy villages with no apparent reason to visit apart from their beauty and traditional way of life and the fact that they are blessed with natural clear and drinkable water from the mountains.

Kiprianades.

Kiprianades takes its name from the first settlers of the village who came from Cyprus (Kipros). It is one of three villages that feature natural springs in the wet part of the central north area and lies 5 kilometres south of Roda. It contains a beautiful mixture of tumbling down houses and smartly painted ones sitting side by side, like so many of the old traditional villages of Corfu. Each one is different from the next, each one with its own unique style, history and architecture.

As you enter the village, the nearest place to park is a small area elevated above the old pink church of Saint Vasillios. Take a drink of fresh water from the ornate single tap on the apex shaped white stone slab, complete with a basin. Peer down over the wrought iron fence at the church and the houses, as they drop downwards into the distance, whilst undercover of the old tree. There are no shops or a kafeneion here but a walk around the lanes is simply delightful.

The Kiprianades springs are within walking distance but you can drive and park on the road above the track, where the springs are signposted, and walk down. I rode my scooter down the track and it does seem possible to take the car down in dry conditions, but I wouldn't advise it!

Once at the bottom, you will see the pool on the left hand side of the track and the small waterfall spilling into the stream on the right. It is very peaceful here and - unlike the springs at Klimatia - the water flows naturally with no manmade structure. Difficult to photograph as the landowner on the right hand side has erected a three foot wire fence along the top of the bank (I presume to stop tourists walking on the land to get a better view). Well worth a visit. Be sure to take a packed lunch, however, fresh water is provided free of charge... Even in August!

Klimatia.

Klimatia can be found off the main road heading south to Corfu town from the northern resorts of Roda and Acharavi. Turn left after 5 kilometres and follow the country road for a further 3km, where you can park next to the church on the right hand side. The village is a small community of around 300 including surrounding hamlets. There stands the imposing church of Saint George with a bell tower on the opposite side of the road, which is not only unusual but also quite difficult to photograph.

A long walk uphill on an unpaved track above the village will take you to the Holy Trinity Orthodox monastery. Original dates of worship go back to the 14th century and it has a beautiful collection of frescoes and icons from the 17th and 18th centuries. With panoramic views, the monastery is kept by the priests of the house and is rarely visited by tourists. There are no shops here and access to the village is best on foot.

A few minutes drive down the road there is a turning for the Kato Vrisi springs which is signposted. Follow the narrow track down and you will be greeted with a small, odd shaped, concrete construction painted in white.

Cross the small bridge and walk down to the collection of springs that are flowing with fresh water even in August. You can fill your bottles here and take a well earned rest whilst taking in the peace and tranquillity of the countryside. Often you will find you are the only visitors there even at the height of the season. When I visited, there was an abundance of turquoise coloured dragonflies feeding on the giant lily pad leaves. This water rich area in the central north, comprising of Klimatia, Kiprianades and Nimfes, is well worth a visit as there are many rare springs which are literally worth their weight in gold.

Nimfes.

30 kilometres north of Corfu town or 5 kilometres inland from the resort of

Roda, perched on a hill some 200 metres above sea level, is the old village of Nimfes. Legend has it that nymphs have bathed in the waterfalls near here since ancient times and that there are regular sightings, especially in the spring when the rains have filled the area with water. The waterfall is visible in the winter during the rainy months but unfortunately is dry in the summer months. The village has a population of around 750 and the church of Saint Nicholas stands proudly in the square. The yearly festival or Panigiri is on the 8th September. There are also celebrations for Saint Kostandinos on the 21st May and Stavromenos on the 14th September. There are two tavernas and a kafeneion, where you can enjoy a drink or a meal from the daily specials board or just relax under the huge tree on the elevated grassed area with a picnic. Nearby is the Agriculture Co-operative building where they produce the famous kumquat liquor and sweets. Kumquat has been cultivated in China and Japan for centuries and it was brought to Corfu by the English botanist, Merlin, in 1924. It grows particularly well there because of the amount of rainfall in the winter months, the mild climate and the rich soil.

Not far from the village is the small holy monastery of Askitario, where it is said that the monk Artemios Paissios from Epirus, who performed many wonders, lived in the 5th century. The monastery lies 1 kilometre outside of the village and is one of the oldest Christian buildings in Corfu. Legend has it that Artemios lived in seclusion on the site and when his parents came for him, he dug a hole to hide from them and pray as he didn't want to leave. A stone fell and covered the hole whilst he was praying and buried him. His parents then built the monastery of Metamorphoses in his honour. This was my favourite place to take a rest...magical.

My only regret was that we had no serious rain on Corfu since the spring time and therefore the famous waterfalls in Nimfes were dry when I visited.

As I entered Sokraki I parked up and wandered around the tiny streets around the village. When I came back to the main street I decided to have a drink in a café, not in the famous Emily's but the one opposite. It was a tiny café with a front door and a window and stood alone. The walls outside were painted a pastel green and the owner was sitting at a table with two chairs. I hadn't spoken to anyone around the village by this time so I thought this was the perfect chance for a history lesson. I ordered a Ginger beer from the lady inside and sat down to engage with the owner. Of course, he didn't speak any English and why would he. We were high up in the mountains in the lap of the Gods. After half an hour I had enough information about the village and headed for home. The views on the way down the mountain were extraordinary.

Sokraki.

If you ever wondered what it would be like to drive a Ferrari grand prix racing car around a track with hairpin bends, then the drive to this village is for you. I decided to approach the village from the north so that after my visit I could take in the scenery by driving downhill. I wasn't disappointed, the views are magnificent. Most people take the ascent from Ano Korakiana where you will encounter over twenty hairpin bends going uphill to a height of 500 metres on the wrong side of the road! I counted twenty three on the way down.

Rumour has it that the road was built by an Englishman but I can't find anyone to confirm this. The main church is devoted to the Saint Panagia and the local panigiri or festival falls on 15th August. Sokraki is built on Korakio mountain, which lies on the eastern side of the Troumpeta range of mountains which reach a height of 620 metres at Mount Tsouka.

The village is unique as it is famous for its diverse views. Looking south in the morning you can watch the sunrise and see the southern tip of Corfu. Looking north in the evening you can watch the sunset and see the satellite islands of Othoni, Mathraki and Erikousa.

The square is immaculate with crazy paving and well painted buildings. There are a couple of café bars a and a very smart olive wood shop selling tasteful souvenirs. The walls outside the houses are adorned with an eclectic range of pots containing flowers and shrubs. Emily's café is the most famous one in the village for the ginger beer that it serves which is made in the factory at Kalafationes. There are many churches here and one is called "The entry of the most holy Theotokos into the temple"... Try remembering that after a few ouzos!

The next day I travelled over to Agios Markos on my way to meet some friends on the northeast coast at Barbati. Aleko Damaskinos had agreed to meet me in his local kafeneion and said he would write a footnote about the history of Agios Markos which I could include in the book. Aleko is a revered historian of Corfu and a professor of mathematics so it was a privilege to meet him and we are still friends to this day.

Agios Markos.

This village dates back to Venetian times and is a protected area. It is reached from the end of the Ipsos resort through Pirgi and up to the left where there is a left hand turn. Here is the Panorama bar with beautiful views over Ipsos, the sea and beyond. Often misinterpreted as the "Moonjuice bar" or the "Moonshine bar", the Panorama has a reputation for excellent homemade wines. The welcome is engaging, the vista hypnotic, the barrels of local krassi intoxicating. As you amble around the main road you will notice new houses tiered downward and the old village above. Take a walk upwards and you will be amazed at the architecture of the Venetian buildings. Many are deserted and falling down but still show evidence of a rich past. Old mansions, a decrepit church and walkways with tumbling bougainvillea stand alongside and contrast with the renovations. Here lies the Orthodox church of Yperageia Theotokos Lampovitissa (Virgin Mary Lampovitissa); the stunning painting of whom hangs in the Byzantine museum in Athens and was painted between 1610 and 1690. The panigiri is held on 8th September.

Footnote by Aleko Damaskinos.

In the early sixties the villagers were re-housed at the foot of the hill about 3 kilometres away, behind Ipsos beach, because the mountainside subsided in various places. This new settlement is known locally as "the swallower" or "the one that swallows" and it is from here that the underground streams found their way to the village of Agios Markos. The damage to the houses was beyond repair since enormous cracks appeared in the walls and in some cases the foundations slid down the hill. When the villagers were rehoused by the state, they kept their old homes as well as their land. Although the houses are now in a state of total collapse; the olive trees and other fruit trees, that are on the land near their original houses, are still tendered by their owners today.

I didn't get a chance to visit the village of Loutses but still wanted to include it in the book. I simply ran out of time so I asked Bob Giles if he would like to guest write the village where he and Tricia lived. He agreed and also supplied the photographs so with the final piece of the jigsaw I had completed part two of the book. The first book was called "The Hidden Treasures" The second book would be called " The Jewels in the Crown".

The funds had grown due to the sale of the eBook part one and I now had 1,000 euros in the designated payPal account. Bob and Tricia came down to Corfu town again and together with my wife Ann we made a second donation of food to the Red cross. Again the staff met us with big smiles and huge hugs.

Loutses. By Bob Giles.

Loutses is situated to the north of the island, on the eastern side of Mount Pantokrator, some 300 metres above sea level. It commands spectacular views of Mount Pantokrator which dominates the area. From the 'hamlets' of Anapafteria, Karloukia and Zervou there are magnificent views across the Straits of Corfu towards Albania and mainland Greece in the East; The Ionian sea to the North and Corfu town and the Corfiot coastline leading to it to the South. Loutses was once a major village and has had at least two different police stations. (Three if you listen to some!) It was a predominantly agricultural area with olive farming at the fore. If one talks to older residents it becomes clear that there were also vast tracts of grapevines covering that part of the mountainous countryside that was not planted with olives. Many younger family members have moved to the cities, returning only for major holidays. In summer, the population swells with families returning from Athens and elsewhere on the mainland as well as the foreigners who have holiday homes in the locale. It is so different to winter when the major activity still revolves around the olive harvest.

It still sports a taverna and kafeneion. The kafeneion is well worth a visit just to meet the owner, Philipos, a true character and tremendous source of information about the area. The church of Agios Athanasios is active and stands overlooking the village. The 'square' outside the church is home to the annual Panigiri which is held on the last Sunday of July every year. It is probably one of the largest on the island and is very well supported. One local attraction is Loutses caves. To reach it, drive through the village until the road signposted 'Anapafteria' on the left. Take this road and following for a little under a kilometre where there is a turning to the right. Take this turning and follow it. Although it becomes nothing more than a track, it is negotiable by any motor vehicle. The road climbs up and comes to a dead end. From there the cave is a short descent down a footpath.

It was great to have ten days with the family and eating three meals a day. It gave me the strength and energy I needed for my five long days in the north. When I wrote the Central Corfu eBook I didn't eat during the daytime which was a mistake and I learnt from that. Many of the villages don't have a taverna and so unless I took food with me I would go without until I got back to Pelekas. Look after your body and your body will look after you.

This completed my twenty villages of the north of Corfu and when I got home I quickly edited the text and chose the photographs for an earlier release in the October. The second eBook would have one hundred pages and would be in a flip book design where you could flip the pages with your finger on whatever device you had downloaded it on. It was ground breaking at the time and it looked great. I launched it with the slogan, It's bigger, it's better and it's sexier! Well, it's all about marketing isn't it? And in later Blogs I would sign off with Steve Ford...Coming to a village near you!

In October Ann and I took one last week to Corfu as the flight prices were ridiculously cheap and it would make the wait until the following year a bit shorter. Pelekas was quiet now and it was nice to catch up with our Greek friends in the village as August is very busy. The mornings were very fresh but as the sun rose it was still around 25c. We went to the beaches of Ermones, Glyfada, Agios Gordios and Kontogialos (Pelekas) on the west coast and to Ipsos and Dassia on the west coast. At night it was chilly when the sun went down but we had bought warmer clothes and a lovely time to visit. Corfu town was as busy and charming as ever and is a delight at any time of the year for us.

Sitting at home in November I was writing my Corfu villages Blog and thinking about the different charities on Corfu. As many of the people who had bought the book were animal lovers I could make a donation to the Corfu Donkey rescue in Doukades and one to Corfu dogs. I could do this online so I duly sent over 100 euros to both charities and hopefully build up the funds before next years visit.

Chapter 6. Corfu South.

The south is different from the rest of the Island as it is a lot flatter with a fantastic sense of space. It is like going back in time to a place which is largely untouched by tourism.

Here you will still see the donkey used as a mode of transport to carry the daily toil from the fields of labour. This is the traditional part of the Island where the villagers work the land and sea like they have done for centuries.

There is a strong companionship here and the people are fiercely independent. Not surprising when you think that they have borne the brunt of many of the invasions that have beleaguered Corfu over the years.

The villages seem unperturbed by the main Lefkimmi road which cuts through some of their villages like a sharp knife cutting through a piece of sponge cake. They have seen it all before here and just get on with it. They are hardy people and extremely friendly to outsiders. Some speak German, Italian, French and English which is mostly because of the occupation during World War II.

Being at a lower altitude it was much easier to get around on the scooter and although still a long way from my base in Pelekas I found that I could ride down and return in the same day.

What impressed me was the amount of kafenions that still exist in the south. This is where you get to learn about the villages in the area and the true way of life that the locals live. The politics, the hardships and the special times when there is a birthday, wedding, christening or a festival. The kafenions were bursting with people in the early evening shouting to one another from across the square.

Also, in some villages there were trendy cafes too, where the younger ones go for a frappe or a drink during the day and at night. The busy main road in

Agios Mattheos has many tavernas and café bars. Argirades has a mini market, snack bar, fruit shop, café, butcher, electrical shop, hairdresser, clothing shop, scooter shop and more. The villages of Lefkimmi also have many shops too which makes the south somewhat self sufficient and in some ways not so reliant on Corfu town as other areas further north.

The vibrant blue Jacaranda tree by the church in Vraganatika, the kafenion owned by the 87 year old Spiros in Chlomatiana and the fresh fish tavernas at Petriti will remain with me forever.

I would need to visit fourteen villages in the south to complete the trilogy of the three eBooks and once complete I could then release an omnibus edition and eventually a printed version.

Argirades.

Argirades is a large picturesque village situated on the main road south to Lefkimmi and is 33 kilometres south of Corfu Town. The population numbers over 1,000 and was the administrative centre for the Korrision municipality. As you approach the village from the busy main road you are greeted by the mighty church of Agios Ioannis (Saint John). At 100 metres above sea level, there are views from the church of the sea of the west and east coasts. On the opposite side of this road is the main school building, so the children have to cross this road every day during term time. The main road was built some fifteen years ago to link Lefkimmi port and the resort of Kavos in the south with Corfu town via the junction at Messonghi.

There are many festivals and religious celebrations here as Argirades has retained its cultural roots and remains true to its traditions. The festival of the Holy Spirit is held on 24th June at the Holy Trinity church in the heart of the village. The main occupations of the villagers are agriculture and tourism. The nearest resort is the 12km beach at Agios Georgios southwest which is only 2km away on the twisting road downhill from the village. The houses here reflect the influence of the Venetian period, as Argirades was a strategic centre at that time. The name derives from the word Argyros which would have been an important family or persons surname and dates back to Byzantine times.

I drove a car into the village and soon had to turn back as the lanes were so narrow in places, hence the scooter being my means of transport now. Many of the houses are whitewashed and flower pots adorn every ledge. The village was declared a preservation site in 1977 as many of the houses are old. Some of them have now been renovated. A few kilometres north is Lake Korrision which is a must see for those interested in the diverse wildlife of the Island.

Agios Mattheos.

Agios Mattheos is 24 kilometres southwest of Corfu town and is set in beautiful woodland on the hillside of the slopes of Mount Gamilios. The village has 1,600 inhabitants whose main income comes from farming and the collection of olives. As in many villages today, locals also work in the summer months in the nearby tourist resorts of Moraitika and Messonghi.

Another traditional occupation is the cultivation of vineyards, from which they produce the famous kakotrighis wine; a clear, lightly flavoured white wine. The village panigiri is held on 6th August after five days of pilgrimages to the monastery on the top of the hill of the Pantokrator (The Lord). Agios Mattheos is a picturesque village with narrow, winding whitewashed lanes and many traditional coffee shops and tavernas lining the main road. The village is surrounded by a large and dense forest, where the outlaws of the early 19th century used to hide among the myrtle trees and the heather. A paved road leads to the monastery of Pantokrator and the Grava cave. The views from here are magnificent. From Agios Mattheos, a road leads to Paramonas; a fabulous sandy beach surrounded by grey rocks and decorated with a few small rocky islands, further out in the sea. Another road, starting just before the village of Agios Mattheos, leads south to the small and quiet beaches of Prasoudi, Kanouli and Skidi. The beautiful sweeping bay of Alonaki is at the northernmost edge of Korission Lake.

On the road from Agios Mattheos to Chalikounas is where the perennial spring at Gardiki can be found. These springs not only give water to the inhabitants of the area but also to the nearby villages. This area is dominated by the ruins of its Byzantine castle, which was probably built in the 13th century by Michael the II, Despot of Epirus.

My June visit went well and I managed to juggle my time between spending time with my guests and visiting the villages.

The first week we headed down to Benitses to have lunch with friends and then on to explore the old village that lies up the hill. Benitses surprised me as after the boom time of the 70's and 80's had left the resort looking somewhat tired and worn out it was back to its best with a new marina and a smart tree lined front with some very nice tavernas.

The old village was very pretty with bougainvillea and flowers adorning the houses. A little further walk bought us to the water springs and I took some great photos there. Then on to Messonghi and then cross country to the village of Chlomatiana before heading back to Pelekas.

At the weekend I would head down to Lefkimmi to visit the villages in the far south. Ringlades and Potami on Saturday and Perivoli and Vitalades on Sunday. After a couple of days rest a trip to the beautiful village of Vraganiotika in the morning with a lazy afternoon in Vouniatades.

Then to the hilltop village of Stavros then back to Chlomatiana to meet Facebook friend Scarlett "Duchess" Paizanos who took me around the village and to meet the owner of the local kafeneion.

Corfu town was next on my list as I had a couple of letters to be delivered by hand to the head of the Cultural society. The letter was a timetable of events that I am proposing for the "Corfu all Nations day" in aid of Corfu charities I hope to hold in Corfu town next summer. After going to the Town hall I was told I had to go to the Municipality building. There I was told I had to go to the Cultural offices. Eventually I met the right people and handed in the application for the Mayors attention. Fingers crossed I would hear something soon. But this idea would never come to be and that was disappointing as I had many supporters of the idea.

Back in Pelekas I had a meeting with Papa Labbis who is the village Papas but also looks after a large area taking in many villages in what we still call Pareleon. We talked about what the poorest people of the area needed and it was agreed that I would make a donation from the profits from the books which would be used to buy food and medicines for the most needy.

So, another great trip and I had now caught up with the writing of part 3 of the Corfu villages eBook on the south after my disaster at Easter.

Benitses.

A 100 metres up the hill from the resort of Benitses is the old village of the same name, where life goes on as it has always done beside the hustle and bustle of the tourist area. Ruins of Roman baths indicate the age of the village. Though worth seeing, you will have to navigate a few alleyways to find them. The early residents of the village were mainly from the mainland area of Souli in Epirus. In 1537, after the Turks' failed attempts to take Corfu town, they seized 20,000 villagers and sold them to slavers from Egypt and Contantinople. When the Venetians ruled Corfu they repopulated the villages with people from the mainland to work the land. The origin of the name Benitses is shown in documents from the period of the Angevins, before the Venetian period; when in the 13th century the area was referred to as Penitisai, derived from the Ancient Greek "Penio", meaning a place that has rivers and is generally rich in waters. Benitses used to have two small rivers which reached the sea where the harbour is now. This was the main reason for the area's importance over the centuries. Later, the name Penitisai changed over the years into Penitsai and finally into the current Benitses.

The church of Saint Marina is the oldest here and is celebrated on the 16th and 17th July. The festival of Saint John, which has children leaping over a fire on June 22nd, is locally called Lampatines. A third festival is the "Celebration of the Sardine", in recognition of the fishing heritage of the village, which takes place around the first ten days of August. In 1982 a cultural society was set up to preserve the traditional customs of the village and organises events, celebrations and festivals which include music and folklore dancing. During the month of June the annual Achillion race takes place. Starting from the school in Kinopiastes there is a race of 10,000 metres and one of 21,000 metres (half marathon). The athletes come from clubs from all over Greece and Italy to participate and the route takes them through Gastouri, the mountain hills, and finishes in Benitses.

Chlomatiana.

This village lies 25 kilometres south of Corfu town and is easily reached from its nearest resorts of Moraitika and

Messonghi, on the south east coast. It is a small village with a population of around 250 and is said to be the sister village of Chlomos, just few kilometres south. The church on the hill is devoted to the Panagia Kasopitra and from here you can look out over the village below. The panigiri or festival takes place on the 8th May.

The plateia or square is elevated from the road and surrounded by houses, both lived in and empty, on three sides. There is a fresh water tap for those who want to freshen up or take a drink, which is advisable as there are no shops here. Many tourists come here to visit the Archontiko (mansion) restaurant. The views of the mountains and the sea are great from here: couples come from long and far for a romantic meal. The place itself is a grand but tasteful new build with a goldfish pool and tendered gardens. You can choose to eat inside or outside depending on the weather.

A walk around the village will bring you to one of the nicest Kafeneions I have been to. I went there to meet a friend of mine Scarlett Blissett Paizanos, who has lived in Corfu for 27 years and had agreed to show me around her adopted village. I arrived 10 minutes early and was greeted by the 87 year old owner Spiros, who served me with an ice cold beer. I told him that I was from Pelekas and we talked in Greek about what I was doing there and where he had a shop some years ago, near Agios Gordios. With the help of a map and every Greek word I know I stumbled through until my interpreter arrived.

Scarlett then asked Spiros about the history of the village and he said that the Italians had been stationed there during the World War 2. The rest is history as they say.

Ringlades.

The town of Lefkimmi is 40 kilometres south of Corfu town and is not really a town at all. With a population of around five thousand it is the second largest inhabited area on the Island. It has evolved over centuries and is made up from the five villages of Anaplades, Ringlades, Agioi Theodoroi, Potami and Melikia. Ringlades is said to be the first of the settlements of Lefkimmi and has Byzantine roots. The name comes from the Ringli family who lived in the area in the Middle Ages.

The churches of Agioi Anayiri and Agios Arsenios both stand on the main road and differ from many churches in Corfu as they both have twin belfries, centre windows and arches.

There is an active philharmonic band, choir and dance group who lead the parade at the yearly panigiri festival on 15th August. At Easter (Paska), Ringlades holds a "pot throwing" ceremony on Saturday morning where the locals, dressed in traditional dress, throw clay pots from the balconies of their houses to cast away evil spirits.

Anaplades village has been absorbed by Ringlades; which was first settled by Venetian refugees and soldiers in the 1540s, when the Turks conquered Nafplio (Anapli).

The long road through the villages is at sea level and flat. There are single, double and three story houses that line the narrow road. There is an eclectic mix of derelict buildings next door to new with a sprinkle of shops mixed in between selling clothes and home style goods. There are also a supermarket, pharmacy, bakery, car work shops and trendy café bars.

Potami.

As you drive through Lefkimmi from Ringlades you will arrive at the village of Potami. You will recognise it immediately, as the road takes you to a picturesque bridge over the river of the same name. Mentioned in the archives since 1618; the river used to be the main transport of agricultural produce to the sea, Corfu town and the Greek mainland. With the improvement of the road network from the start of tourism in the 1970's, the port has gradually declined. The river draws its water from the Lefkimmi plains and flows into the sea at the small untouched local beach of Bouka, a 15 minute walk away. Fishing and leisure boats line the banks either side of the river all year round and there are tavernas and cafés on all four sides of the bridge. You will often see the locals dangling a line over the edge to catch the fish that swim lazily below. A short drive away is the beach at Alikes and the Lefkimmi salt flats. Natural sea salt has been cultivated here since the 15th century, under the watchful eye of the old lighthouse which has guided sailors here for centuries.

Melikia is the last of the villages of Lefkimmi, whose name derives from the Meliki family who first settled in the 15th century. The church of Agios Isavros has many fine frescoes and icons dating back to the 16th century. Traditionally Greek and mostly untouched by tourism, this is a beautiful part of the Island. There are rooms to rent but very few. Here you will see the local women wearing traditional clothing and a headdress, often using donkeys to carry the collection from a days toil in the fields.

This is the old Corfu. The very reason that we came here in the first place and the reason we come back, year after year. Life here goes on like it has for centuries. From here the road leads to the port of Lefkimmi where you can take the ferry to Igoumenitsa. A further drive south will bring you to the lively resort of Kavos.

After a full day out I drove the one hour journey back to Pelekas. I had intended to stay in the south for a couple of nights but once again it didn't work out as there is very little accommodation in the villages but on reflection, maybe I should of stayed in Agios Georgios (Saint George south). Anyway, the next day I set of for the villages of Perivoli and Vitalades. After a good nights sleep the 35 kilometre road down was nice and peaceful. Riding down the flat plains down the lower part of the Island was a much easier ride than the hilly central area and the mountainous north. In all my years visiting Corfu I had never really ventured to the southern parts of the Island and if anyone says to you that Corfu is commercial, tell them to go south of the Island and they will be surprised just how traditional it is.

Perivoli.

Perivoli is 35 kilometres south of Corfu town and just 5 kilometres north of Lefkimmi, sitting 30 metres above sea level. It has a population of over 1400 so is considered a large village. The land around here is flatter and therefore ideal for farming and there are many vineyards and olive groves. Being so close to the sea there are fishermen here too.

The main churches here are Agios Saranda and Agios Theodoros and a large festival is held in commemoration of the Transfiguration of Jesus on 6th August.

Many villages are deserted in the daytime when the locals are at work in the fields or the resorts but come alive in the evening. Perivoli is one such village. When I visited on a summer evening I was amazed at the amount of people that were in the cafés and bars. A hundred eyes followed me as I took photographs of the church, the houses and the cafés. The square echoed with the banter of the locals who chatted and called to one another from café to bar and taverna.

There is a mini market, a yellow periptero (kiosk that sells tobacco, soft drinks and ice cream etc.) cafés, bars and a few tavernas; all in the centre. It is a true hub of activity and many of the larger villages of the south, from Agios Mattheos down to Lefkimmi, seem to have similar local evening get togethers. The nearest beach is just over 1km east at Kaliviotis, where many of the villagers keep their small fishing boats in the small harbour. To the west are the beautiful sandy beaches of Vitalades and Santa Barbara.

The nearest resorts are Kavos in the south and Agios Georgios south west.

Vitalades.

40 kilometres south of Corfu town and just 4km from Lefkimmi is the traditional village of Vitalades. The main occupations for the population, of around 530, are fishing and agriculture. The fish is caught daily and served in

the tavernas of Vitalades or Gardenos beach, nearby.

The festival takes place on 29th June in honour of the Apostles, Saint Peter and Saint Paul. There is also a 15th century monastery just outside the village, dedicated to Saint Panteleimon, where a second celebration is held on 27th July. From the village, there is a road that will take you down to the beautiful sandy beach of Gardenos; where you can hire sunbeds and a parasol. The back drop is dramatic here, with the hills behind standing guard over the bay like a green blanket. There are three tavernas here and all of them offer fresh fish; caught locally, the same day. There is a café bar nearby and a taverna on the hill with fantastic views of the sea and the sunset. There is also a small harbour, where the locals keep their fishing boats. Here there is mud or clay underfoot which the villagers cover themselves with, allow to dry, then wash off, to leave themselves with smooth skin. There is a mini market in the village as well as a couple of kafenions and a grill room which does pizza, to eat in or take away.

I visited in the early evening on a summer's night. The men had put square tables on the road opposite the kafenion and the grill room/pizzeria and sat on white plastic chairs. Here they would debate the issues of the day while drinking beer, ouzo or coffee and would call over the road for a plate of souvlaki. The women were on the other side of the road sitting outside their houses, probably talking about the men! This is a very calm, pretty village where life hasn't changed much for many a year... thank the Lord.

For a change everything was going to plan and after a couple of days rest I travelled to the now shorter distances to the villages of Chlomos and Stavros on the way back. When I reached Chlomos I was really thirsty. It was a hot day and I had already drunk my bottle of water that I had bought from home by the time I had arrived. I went into the taverna in the main street and looked for an ice lolly but all they had was chocolate covered Magnum ice creams. I bought one, ordered a frappe and sat down at a table opposite the taverna. I really didn't want to eat chocolate as it was so hot and there was an ashtray on the table so I peeled off all the chocolate and put it in the ashtray. The ice cream was delicious but when my frappe arrived the waitress stared in amazement at the pool of melted milk chocolate laying in the ashtray. I didn't know the Greek words for "Sorry but I wanted a lollypop" But I think she got the message. (Signomi thelo lollypop?) Or, "I don't like chocolate" (Then moresi chocolate?) On the next table and the only other tourists there was a young couple. He was Portuguese and she was English. They had met at Stafford university and knew the area where I lived in Wolverhampton. It's a small World.

Chlomos.

Chlomos is an old village dating back to the 13th century. The brother of

Thomas Palaiologos, the last Byzantine despot, lived here and there are a few remains of a 14th century church. Chlomos means "Pale of face". The original villagers lived down on the land by Issos beach and were ravaged by sickness, malaria and pirate raids so were "very pale". So, they moved up the mountainside to settle where they are now and these days are a little darker in complexion!

The village lies 30 kilometres south from Corfu Town on the Lefkimmi road and sits 330 metres up on mount Kavalovouni with views to the sea on the west and east coasts. It is a quiet village with a few tavernas, a church and a population of around 500.

The views from the Orthodox church of Taxiarchai at the top of the hill are spectacular and well worth a visit. To the east there are views of the coast, the Ionian sea and the Greek mainland and to the west there are views of the coast and the Adriatic sea. The houses are grouped together with no room for extensions so some of the residents have built upwards and many now have a third floor or attic which is unusual outside of Corfu town.

Many of the houses are painted in pastel which brings a pleasing and relaxing sense of colour to the village. Photos taken at the top of the village looking down take in the ochre tiled rooftops of the houses.

The streets here are very narrow, especially in the centre so it is best to park the car in the car park at the edge of the village. You have been warned!

Vraganiotika.

Just off the Lefkimmi main road 25 kilometres south of Corfu town is the lovely village of Vraganiotika. It has a population of around 260 and sits at 40 metres above sea level. The village is one of the oldest in the south and was populated as the nearby Gardiki settlement declined. The word Vragka is a Slavic word for enemy. The enemy was malaria so the people looked inland for higher, drier ground.

The newly painted, deep pink church of Agios Paraskevi is flanked at one end with purple bougainvillea. Pots and trays of geraniums, hydrangeas and different coloured flowers reside all around the church ground walls. What I believe is a vibrant light blue Jacaranda tree, greets you as you walk up the small lane to the church gate. There are oleander bushes and lemon trees lining the lanes that lead off the small square.

The panigiri village festival takes place over two days on 25th & 26th July with the saint's day being on 26th. There are no shops here but local resident Maggie Stamatelou told me that on the main road there is an authentic Greek taverna. Next door there used to be a barbers that one tourist thought was so good, he used to wait until he came to Corfu to have his hair cut. Unfortunately the barber passed away a few years ago. On the other side of the taverna is a hunting shop which is also the post office. Here the "best postman" Giorgos will send you a message on Facebook if you have any post and at Christmas will offer to stick the stamps on your cards, before posting. Next to the post office is Spiros's café bar where the men play cards in the evening. Nearby is the Mavroudis modern olive press where they are in the process of creating a museum which will house a collection of old machinery and methods of oil production. This is a beautifully quaint, small village and is close to the resorts of Moraitika and Messonghi. Visit this village and, believe me, you will be rewarded for your efforts.

Vouniatades.

Although historical records from the south date back to the 14th century, there is evidence that the rulers from Epirus were there in the 13th century. Villages such as Vouniatades, Vragionatika and Chlomatiana may even have a history going back as far as 1000 AD. The villages in this area were populated on the hills for security and to escape piracy but also for a clean water supply, from the nearby mountains. Vouniatades is a small pretty village with lovely views to the hillside villages of Ano and Kato Pavliana and Kato Garouna. Just north of Agios Mattheos, the nearest resort is Agios Gordios west. It is perched on a hill at 100 metres above sea level and has a population of around 240. The church here is the Orthodox church of Saint John.

The village festival is held on 24th June and although the village is small it attracts locals from all the neighbouring villages, as they have a live band and of course lamb on the spit. The panigiri here goes on until the early hours of the morning.

Whenever I go southwest from Pelekas I use the road that leads through Vouniatades and always stop for a break and a walk around the small square. The road winds up to the village and down again like a snake: many people go through and must think that it is a nice village, without having a thought to stop. This summer I passed through in the light warm evening sun and stopped at the café, for a drink and a talk with the locals.

Do you want to practice your Greek language? Then this is a great place to come and have a coffee or an ouzo with the locals and walk around the village to view the surrounding countryside and nearby hilltop villages.

Stavros.

The Byzantine village of Stavros lies 220 metres above sea level and approximately 12 kilometres south of Corfu town and has a population of around 450. As you pass the impressive large white church on your right, you will arrive at the main street where there is a taverna and an old British red telephone box. The panigiri here is on the 15th August and on the evening before there is a procession around the village and afterwards plates of macaroni are offered, to all that take part. There is also the festival of the Holy Spirit which falls on 24th June.

Mount Stavros stands above the village at 435 metres and Stavros takes its name from the Greek word for cross. It is believed that warning cloth flags were hung from the wooden cross, whenever pirates were seen approaching the coast. Others believe that the wooden cross was used as a deterrent towards pirate invasions by signalling to the pirates that they would be punished by crucifixion, if they attempted to attack the villagers.

Around 1700 a village built at the foot of a mountain was completely destroyed by pirates and its inhabitants were forced to move up the hill. The village which was the first settlement in the Stavros area was called Gouloumata. It is believed that it was settled by a community from the island of Cephalonia. When the pirates came into sight the villagers hid themselves in a cave, on a steep slope on the mountain. The pirates followed them and tried to get into the cave but as the slope was very steep and the entrance of the cave was very narrow they were forced to climb up one at the time and the villagers were able to kill them as they attempted to reach the cave. The pirates then decided to use gun powder barrels to blow up the cave. There are still big rocks scattered near the entrance of the cave which seems to confirm the legend. The cave today is called the burnt cave "kammeni grava".

Stavros.

The Byzantine village of Stavros lies 220 metres above sea level and approximately 12 kilometres south of Corfu town and has a population of around 450. As you pass the impressive large white church on your right, you will arrive at the main street where there is a taverna and an old British red telephone box. The panigiri here is on the 15th August and on the evening before there is a procession around the village and afterwards plates of macaroni are offered, to all that take part. There is also the festival of the Holy Spirit which falls on 24th June.

Mount Stavros stands above the village at 435 metres and Stavros takes its name from the Greek word for cross. It is believed that warning cloth flags were hung from the wooden cross, whenever pirates were seen approaching the coast. Others believe that the wooden cross was used as a deterrent towards pirate invasions by signalling to the pirates that they would be punished by crucifixion, if they attempted to attack the villagers.

Around 1700 a village built at the foot of a mountain was completely destroyed by pirates and its inhabitants were forced to move up the hill. The village which was the first settlement in the Stavros area was called Gouloumata. It is believed that it was settled by a community from the island of Cephalonia. When the pirates came into sight the villagers hid themselves in a cave, on a steep slope on the mountain. The pirates followed them and tried to get into the cave but as the slope was very steep and the entrance of the cave was very narrow they were forced to climb up one at the time and the villagers were able to kill them as they attempted to reach the cave. The pirates then decided to use gun powder barrels to blow up the cave. There are still big rocks scattered near the entrance of the cave which seems to confirm the legend. The cave today is called the burnt cave "kammeni grava".

This turned out to be a very successful trip and I had managed to visit ten villages. With the two villages I had been to in April it meant I only had to go to Marathias and Petriti in August. I had a fifteen day holiday booked for the main summer holiday and I headed out first with Ann, Eva and Bobby to follow for their ten days. We had many guests arriving at different times during the holiday so apart from one last day on the road to complete the eBook on the south, this would be the first proper family holiday for three years.

I had asked Ann if she would like to come with me on the final village day out because I wanted her to see the fishing village of Petriti and it would give us a chance to ride back up the east coast road to Benitses.

On the day we cut across from Pelekas through Gastouri and down the winding road to Benitses. We grabbed a coffee and began our second leg of the journey that I had been looking forward to all year. I took the motorway road I call it from Messonghi down to Marathias as it is a quick way and it would give us plenty of time to have lunch in Petriti.

Marathias

"The Plague" by Aleko Damaskinos.

For the second time since 1629 the plague appeared again at Lefkimmi in 1815 because of some illegal merchandise that arrived from an infested part of the world. The nearby village of Marathias was totally burnt down and on Corfu we still have the saying, "Like Marathias" for anything that is completely burnt down! The market at Lefkimmi was guarded by soldiers and the market opened when a yellow flag was raised at 8.00 am in the morning and closed at sunset when the flag was lowered. Whoever passed near this area and did not answer the military command, "Who goes there?" was shot without any further questions and any dog or other animal which approached the area was killed on the spot! From the 1st November 1815 until 15th June 1816, 414 people died and 1,031 were infected by the disease until it was officially announced that this terrible disease was no longer a threat.

A few kilometres south of Argyrades, on the main Lefkimmi road, there is a well known upmarket restaurant, on the entrance to the main street to the village. The street meanders along until it brings you back to the main road after a few hundred metres. All the houses are on different levels with singles and doubles side by side. Many of the two story houses have a second floor balcony; creating a canopy of shade for the owners, who sit underneath on the ground floor at their outdoor table and chairs. Off the main street, the houses tumble down the hill towards the church. Many of these houses seem to have been built sympathetically, around the olive trees, giving the tree a pride of place and respect. There is a lovely kafeneion, with a couple of tables outside. There is an insurance office adjacent to it, where there is a road which will take you past the main church and down to the beautiful sandy Marathias beach.

From Marathias we went a little further south as I wanted to show Ann the village of Perivoli and from there we could take the coast road back up to Petriti. As we reached the sea we unwittingly stumbled across a small beach with one taverna. I checked the map and found out that we were in Kaliviotes. We were on the Alikes bay and could see the Cape Lefkimmi headland to our right. The sea was as calm and still as I had ever encountered on Corfu so we decided to order a coffee from the taverna and sit on the beach for a while. To our left was children's play area and a concrete jetty with a few small boats. To our right was an upside down rowing boat freshly painted in bright light blue which was sitting underneath a eucalyptus tree. This was one of those moments where we just sat and admired the beauty and tranquillity of the place without words. As a self professed promoter of Corfu I try not to tell people what my favourite villages or beaches are because to me they are all beautiful in their own way but Kaliviotes definitely made an impression on the both of us. We were feeling hungry now so off to Petriti we went for the best and freshest fish tavernas on the Island.

Petriti.

In ancient times the village of Petriti was known as "Egrypos" which derives from the Greek word "Evrous" and literally means good river.The area belonged to a Byzantine landowner by the name of Petretino or Petriti, who granted the village to the Palatianos family as a possible dowry. There is a Byzantine tower, remaining intact, that is believed to still belong to the family. The foundations date back to Roman times and the structure, which is five metres in diameter, is thought to have been a cistern or a grain store. Petriti has been largely populated by the nearby hilltop village of Kourakades, whose houses suffered landslides. The harbour is bustling with fishing boats and boasts to be the largest fishing village in Corfu today. There is a large car park where you can park up for the day and take your pick from seven fish tavernas; who serve fresh fish caught a few hours before, by the local fishermen.

As you head away from the harbour there is an imposing church at ground level which is unusual in Corfu, as most of them are perched high above at the top of the village. A right hand turn will take you up to the centre of the old village, where most of the 700 permanent residents live. There are several festivals here including one to honour Agia Kerkyra at the Orthodox church. The main panigiri is celebrated on 15th August for the Assumption of the Virgin Mary. Petriti is unique as it is a working village on the coastline. The Varkarola is celebrated on 9th August where everyone and anyone take out their boats into the harbour and light candles. I was told that Petriti has the oldest house in Corfu. Set back from the sea, the small chapel there has its name day on 2nd July. The house belonged to the Palationas family and one of the daughters married a British high commissioner, in Victorian times. It is believed that the house is now owned by the Voulgareos family who own the relics of Saint Spyridon.

When I got home I set about compiling the final eBook and it would be called "The Forgotten Treasures". I released it in the October and followed up with the promised omnibus edition. Some people bought the trilogy and others bought the omnibus but the feedback I was getting was that a lot of people wanted a hardback version and so did I.

Chapter 7. The Corfu villages printed book & Charities.

In November I contacted a printer to get some costings and I set to work on the design of a printed edition. I wanted the book to be tourist friendly and I also wanted it to be bold in design and appealing to all ages of children. The thought of releasing a printed book about the villages of Corfu was very exiting and had never been done before which made it even more special. The book had taken three years and twelve holidays to complete. I had travelled to over one hundred villages and had covered over 3,500 kilometres. I would have to invest £1500 of my own money to have the book printed but it was a calculated gamble because I knew there was an audience out there just waiting to buy it. I gave the printer a deadline as I wanted to release the book at the end of November so that I could take advantage of the Christmas trade. Everything went well with the design but the text on many of the villages was too long so I had to edit them which I wasn't very happy about. We hit the deadline and the book was released as planned. It sold well on the dedicated Corfu villages website and when I released it on Amazon the sales were taken to a different level. By Christmas time the PayPal account had swollen considerably and it was at this point I realised that I could make a big difference to the Corfu charities. I had heard about a children's home in Corfu town that was state owned but where the house was run on a shoe string and there were very little privileges for the children. Now I had bigger funds I would be able to make a real difference to a very worthy cause.

I sat at home in January and February, "The Dark Days" I call them, and advertised the printed book on all of my Facebook groups and everyone else's too. I must have driven everyone mad with my constant charity posts but it worked and I make no apology for it. I thank the administrators of all the groups for being so understanding and all the members who have bought the book to this day.

In May 2015 I headed to Corfu once more but I would be on a different mission now. I had asked Claire Richie from Delfini transport if they would take out two boxes of books for me to Corfu containing two hundred books. I would then place some with Alex Christou in Arillas, some with Sally Tinkler at her bar in Ipsos, the English shop near Perama and some with Rodula Kontis at the Hawaii pool bar in Pelekas. This meant that anyone who lived on Corfu could buy the book and I could collect the money if and when I was around those areas. This proved to be a little difficult going forward as I became quite busy with the charities so I decided to have the books in Pelekas only in the future. Don't get me wrong, the books sold well on Corfu but in the end I told them to keep the money and donate it to a local cause of their choice and they were happy to do it.

I met with a Greek friend, Reni Doika who introduced me to the lady who runs the children's home in Analipses which is next door to the Mon Repos estate. I asked Kiria Vicky as I call her what was needed at the house and how could I help. At this point I realised how proud and humble the Greek people are after a good discussion we made a plan.

I organised a book signing on the Liston in Corfu town and invited everyone I new who lived on the Island and anyone who was on holiday at the time. I was a bit unsure about the book signing as although I had written a book about Corfu I was not an author or a professional writer. I was a tourist who loved the Island and wanted to do what I could to help the Corfiot people. The meeting went well and I sold some books and met some lovely people. This would become a regular meeting over the next few years as it was a good opportunity to meet people from the Corfu charities and like minded tourists too.

By June the sales of the book had reached £5,000 so I emailed the children's home and asked them to give the children a "wish list". I told Vicky that if the children had a wish in their deepest dreams what would they want. The children have nothing but the basics so this would be a real treat. I had an email back to ask for six bicycles, five mobile phones and a play station. Vicky had told the children that there was an Englishman who had written a book about the villages of

Corfu and he wanted to donate the profit he had made from the sale of the book to the house and the children.

The ages of the children at the home range from around four to eighteen and Vicky, who was a child at the home herself when she was young, are from broken homes and come from all over Greece and not just from Corfu.

My wife Ann and I arrived late on the 8th July and headed to Pelekas village for a few drinks and to meet our European and Greek friends. The following day we met with my friend Reni and we went to Corfu town to pay for the bicycles for the children's home and to arrange delivery for the following week. In the evening we ate at the Hawaii pool bar as they have a Greek night every Thursday with a BBQ and Greek dancing. Food shopping the following day was proceeded by a live band in the top of the village. The local children's group danced first and then a Norwegian band played on the steps of Saint Nicholas church at the upper part of the village. The band are regular visitors to Pelekas and they played until the early hours. The next two days we went to Yialiskari and Kontogialos beaches and on Saturday night there was a dance festival in the village square with over 100 dancers from all over Greece. One group had come from the south of Italy and sang songs from the past, some tragic and some joyous, as they told of their history about living in Greece, leaving Greece and settling in Italy. They talked and sang in Greek!

Yes, Pelekas is a busy village at this time of year!

On Sunday I said to Ann we had to go to the village after the morning church service as I needed to see the Papas to make a donation to the Paralion as he does a lot of work for the poorer people in the surrounding villages, the blood bank and the hospital. I asked her to put a dress on and some makeup and we would meet him in the café next door and then go to his office next to the church. What I didn't tell her was that I had organised a "Blessing" in the church a couple of months previously to celebrate our 25th wedding anniversary. It was a very special moment, I hadn't invited or told anyone about it and afterwards when we had made the donation we sat in the café with the papas with a huge smile on our faces.

Afterwards we met with a few people as it was a friends birthday. As we all arrived on scooters we toiled with the idea of starting a Corfu scooter club. The following week we met at the Paradisos taverna opposite Aqualand and enjoyed a traditional English scooter breakfast of bacon and sausage rolls. The idea was to meet every Sunday when we were all there together for a ride out to the villages, have a coffee, have a beer and spend some money in the local kafeneion. The first stop was to Liapades where the locals looked bemused to see 4 Mods riding into their village with their wives on the back and all wearing target and union jack helmets. We shared stories with them in "Gringlish" for an hour then headed off to Doukades for a while before returning back to Agios Ioannis for a beer. It was a great way to spend a Sunday.

After a few lazy days Ann and I took a trip to the Corfu Donkey Rescue centre near Doukades to meet Judy who had started the sanctuary in 2009. We were shown around by Christos the manager who told us that the centre was founded to stop unwanted, old and sick Donkey's from being exported to the Italian meat markets. The volunteers do a wonderful job there and I promised a donation of 275 euros from the profits of the Corfu villages books.

I had a phone call to say that the bicycles were ready for delivery so I went with Reni my Greek friend to the bicycle shop in Corfu town and we bought the bikes. Alex the owner met us a few days later at the home and delivered the bikes with a promise to service them in the future free of charge. Rene had taken delivery of the mobile phones and the play station so we had a photo shoot outside the house it was just like Christmas day. Some of the children were at school at the time of the delivery but the two youngest girls were there and to see the delight on their faces when they were handed their pink bicycles with stabilisers was a sight to behold and a very special moment for me which I will never forget. So I had spent 1,550 euros for the children's gifts and 300 euros to the Papas for food and medical supplies for the area of Paralion.

When I arrived back in the UK I started to make a plan for what I could do next for the children's home. When we were shown around the home in July the boys and girls bedrooms were stiflingly hot and I had wondered how they could sleep at night. Vicky said that it was a problem so I suggested buying an air conditioning unit with a heating option for the winter when I returned. As our last holiday was not until September I decided to make some donations online. I sent the 275 euros I had promised to Judi at the Donkey rescue, 275 euros to Sue Done at the Corfu dogs home and 200 euros to the "Smile of the Child" in the northwest children's home in Magoulades.

I travelled alone in September for a week on my own and Ann would join me for the second week and our last visit of the year. After a couple of days rest in the village I had a surprise invitation to a Greek Christening from my friend Nick Diavatos from Vatos. The service took place at the main church in Evropouli in the centre of the Island. This village isn't featured in the book but it is a lovely village with a couple kafeneion's and an imposing church. It was an emotional afternoon and I felt very privileged to have been one of the few foreigners to attend. The baby's name is Leonidas which means "lion" in Greek. Leonidas was a Spartan king of the 5th century BC who sacrificed his life defending the pass of Thermopylae from the Persians. The service was followed by a party at the father in laws house with Greek pop music, dancing, home made red wine and lamb from the spit. This went on until late into the night and was my kind of party!

The weather was quite good with most days a mixture of sunny and cloudy days so a friend from Gastouri picked me up and we drove to the children's home as there was a threat of rain in the air. Kim had a T.V. that he wanted to donate to the home and when we got there we were greeted by one of the carers and the youngest girl in the house. She was six years old with dark brown hair, dark skin and the whitest teeth you have ever seen. When she saw the T.V. she gave the biggest smile you could imagine and that is what makes giving so worthwhile.

Ann arrived on the Friday night flight and last minute arrangements were made for my birthday party at the Hawaii pool bar in Pelekas on the following day. What we hadn't realised was that England were playing Australia in the rugby World cup. So what was intended to be a get together for twenty people turned out to be a very busy night. There was a tray of moussaka, a tray of chicken from the oven, Greek potatoes, salad, homemade wine and an overnight visit from Sal and Andy Mason from Bristol who came down from Kalami.

A couple of days later we took a trip on the scooter over to Sally's bar in Ipsos. Sally and the staff had raised 240 euros in donations from the sale of the Corfu villages printed book. It was a fantastic achievement and another example of the great work people are doing on Corfu.

The last excursion on the calendar was a meeting with some great people from the Facebook groups, the Corfu Grapevine, Corfu dogs and Friends of Corfu on the Liston. We had a brainstorming session of how we could all help the Corfu charities in the future whilst the rain lashed down and the wind beat upon the umbrellas above our heads. The money raised by Sally was given to the Friends of Corfu group to buy blankets for the hospital as Martin was told that they could only accept new ones and they could not take blankets that had been donated.

It had been another very successful trip apart from the fact that I hadn't been able to buy an air conditioning unit for the children's home. The reason for this was that all of the electrical stores had completely sold out in the hot summer. I stayed positive though and after the winter I would have enough money to but two units. One for the boys bedroom and one for the girls.

Autumn and winter came and went and I took my first Ryanair flight from Birmingham to Corfu for the Greek Paska (Easter). I arrived on Thursday and had planned to ride down to Ringlades in Lefkimmi on Easter Friday and stay the night. It would give me an early start where I could get a good view and a position on the steps of the Agios Arseneos church. On Easter Saturday over 2,000 people from the five nearby villages meet to watch the

"Pot throwing". It is the second largest pot throwing event outside Corfu town and I had to see it. Well of course it rained. What is it about Lefkimmi and me? I gave up and went up to the village to drown my sorrows. I told a Norwegian friend, Ellen, that Zeus had sent the rain to hinder me and she said, " Don't worry, I will take you to Lefkimmi tomorrow and we can go early in the morning". We met at 8.00 am and had time to stop for a Greek coffee in Vouniatades. This was the oldest and most run down kafenion I had ever been to. The old lady was very old and wore an black apron over a heavy brown dress. She walked in heavy black shoes with black stockings and her white hair was flowing at the sides of her traditional headwear. The coffee was awful but at 1.50 euro for a small cup and a bottle of water we didn't have the heart to complain. From the outside of the Kafeneion it was a picture to behold. The old brown double wooden door stood ajar with faded white metal ironwork protecting the upper glass frosted windows and above was the old hand painted shop sign. "Kafepantopoleion" which is basically a shop where you can buy anything. As the clouds began to clear the skies became a deep bright blue and the bright red bougainvillea burst out with colour at the side of the door reaching for height. Underneath the red leaves lay a white flowering Jasmine which gave off the most amazing scent as we sat at the old wooden table covered with a faded checked tablecloth in our red plastic chairs. We arrived in good time in Ringlades at took our position on the steps of the church and to the side of the local choir. The older men were dressed in black suits with a white shirt and a wine coloured Dickie bow. The younger ones wore a black suit, a white shirt and no tie. The ladies wore a black suit, a white blouse, open at the neck with a wine coloured silk scarf. The choir sang with the accompaniment of different instruments until the arrival of the philharmonic brass playing bands from the different villages arrived by marching through the main street. Then at exactly 10.30 am "Pame, pame tora" Let's go, let's go now! The Corfu red coloured pots were thrown from the second floor balconies by the local women in their traditional dress. We were handed a small basket by a local lady which contained a few chocolate eggs. We had a decent frappe from one of the many fashionable café bars in the village and just gazed for a while at this gathering of Greeks with no apparent concern for the "crisis". Everyone was dressed in their Sunday best and this was an uncommercial display of which I have never seen on Corfu before. This is Corfu south.

We drove back to Pelekas and got ready for the Saturday night celebrations. An evening walk around the village streets with the Holy "Lambada" candle and then down to the square where the Papas will announce that "Xristos anesti" (Christ has risen) Where you will reply "Alithos anesti" (He has truly risen) It is a custom to carry the Eternal Flame home and use it to make the sign of the cross on the door frame in smoke. The smoke cross is left there throughout the year, symbolizing that the light of the Resurrection has blessed the home. The fireworks begin and the party starts going into the early hours and the band play on and on.

It made me laugh when I when I entered the saying "Alithos anesti" on Google translate. It read "He really got up".

On Easter Sunday Nick from Vatos picked me up in his WV Golf and we drove to his brothers house at Alykes Potamos for the big lunch. When we arrived his brother Babis was cooking the 25kg lamb and the aroma greeted us we walked down the drive. His wife Maria came to the door to meet us and offered us a home made bottle of wine and Nick and I sat down as honoured guests. Babis owns a large fishing boat and supplies the tavernas on the south east coast with fresh fish daily. Maria's family own a fish stall at the new market in Corfu town. The brothers had a lot to talk about so I took a walk around the grounds. The garden was well tendered and full of young trees. There was an orange tree, a few lemon trees, a pomegranate tree, a fig tree and several olive trees. Herbs were set out in orderly rows and flowers were potted around. The views to the east looked over the valley to the Greek mainland and the Islands of Lazeretto a Vido. Family and friends came and went and it was then I realised that the lamb being cooked was for just four of us! We sat down at the table where there was Greek salad, bread, wine and enough food to feed the village, then Babis entered with the biggest silver tray of cut lamb I have ever seen. The tray was piled high with hot meat with a smell of garlic and rosemary. I helped myself to salad and meat and the trio looked at me and smiled. Maria asked me if I didn't like lamb and I replied "yes, I love it" She then doubled my portion so that my plate was piled as high as the Pantokrator mountain. After the meal Maria said I eat like a pontiki (mouse) but I was bursting and then she bought a huge cake to the table. It looked like a blackberry forest gateau Greek style with extra cream on top.

Nick reached over and knocked over a glass of red wine which travelled like a stream to the edge of the table and over the side down to the white rug underneath. Babis and I stifled our giggles as Maria was not a happy bunny. I offered to clean up by dabbing the wine with kitchen roll and it gave me the opportunity to opt out of the giant sweet. It was a privilege to go to a Greek family home for Easter Sunday and although I didn't understand most of the conversation, Nick would periodically turn to me and tell me what they were talking about and then I would be able to join in. I did surprise Maria though before we left when I spoke Greek from the subtitles on the television. She said if I could read and write Greek why couldn't I understand the conversations at the table? I said I could understand some of it but you talk so fast and with so many Greek people speaking English on Corfu it was difficult especially when I only visit for a few weeks a year. "Katalaves fili mou"? (Do you understand my friend) "Katalava file mou" (I understand my friend) she said.

After a couple of days of cloud and rain I didn't do much but on Wednesday Nick and I went to Corfu town where I had arranged another Corfu villages book meeting on the Liston. We had a great turn out and I met friends from Facebook and from around Corfu. Some who were living on the Island and some who were on holiday. There were some generous donations and I sold some more books so another successful afternoon. We then went to the Konsovolos electrical store where, at last, we ordered two air conditioning units for the boys and girls bedrooms at the children's home. It was good to have Nick with me as although the staff speak very good English he was able to negotiate a discount and a free fitting of the units.

I had a couple of days left to tour and the weather had picked up with the sun now finally deciding to stay for a while. I woke up early the next day and jet washed the dust off the scooter ready for my trip to the Angelokastro (Castle of Angels) in the north west. On my last visit to Krini, the village close by, I had viewed the castle from the hill opposite and promised myself that I would return one day to climb the steep hill to the top. As I reached Krini I stopped for a coffee in the local Kafeneion and sat on the wall under the tree where the two old ladies had giggled and posed for my photograph when writing the Corfu north eBook. There is something special about the villages that keep me coming back, maybe I have unfinished business I don't know. Maybe I want to know the locals better or am I destined to replace them in the future in my old age?

As I left the village and turned the corner to the mighty Kastro I was as equally impressed as the first time I had seen this landscape. I pulled over in the same spot as I had done before but this time I climbed the ridge and walked around to take some photographs from different angles. The winding road down took me to the car park where there was a café, bar, taverna and a kiosk where I paid 2 euros for the privilege of walking on the same ground as the inhabitants from the 5th century. The walk up was steep but not too bad and there were older people with walking sticks who made it to the top whilst taking a few rests in between. At the top the views are simply stunning. On the east side you can look across the Ionian sea towards Italy and on the west side you look back to Corfu. I sat down for a while to gaze around and pulled out a picnic from my bag. Lunch was a cheese, tomato and onion sandwich with a flask of coffee. This was truly "The Jewel in the Crown"

It was time to go back to England and reflect on another fantastic holiday on a place now I call my second home.

When I got back I was contacted by Bob Bakka who is an estate agent from the Netherlands and holidays on Corfu. He said "Steve, if you had 1,000 euros what would you do with it"? I said, "I would buy an air conditioning for the kitchen at the children's home because the staff had to work in temperatures of over 40c to prepare the meals in the summer" Also, "I would get one for the older boys bedroom" Bob answered back to say that his staff at his company had saved the money from charity fundraiser events already and he wanted to donate the proceeds to the Corfu villages fund.

I didn't take my usual holiday to Corfu in June as a few of us took a five day trip to Toulouse in France. We were there for the European football championships and had managed to get tickets for the Wales v Russia game who were in the same group as England. I had however booked a September return to Corfu with my wife Ann so it was nice to go somewhere different for a change.

We arrived late on Monday 12th September and were met by a friend who took us to Pelekas. As always we dropped off our bags and headed for the village for a few drinks and to catch up with friends. A failed attempt to contact Kiria Vicky on the office phone at the children's home meant a lazy day around the village and a chance to buy some breakfast and food for the fridge. The first day is always spent meeting up with our friends, talking over food and drinks and screeches of horror as we explained we were only on Corfu for a week. Yiati? (Why?) was the response.

On Wednesday Nick Diavatis and I decided to go to the children's home and hope Vicky was there to see what they needed as this would be my last visit until April next year. Luckily she was there and this time we took her mobile number. Vicky doesn't speak any English at all and my Greek is limited so it was good to have Nick as a translator. I asked her how the two air conditioning units were that we had bought for the small children's rooms in the spring and she said that they were fantastic. We told her that a friend from the Corfu Island Facebook group named Bob Bakker from the Netherlands had donated 1,000€ for another two air conditioning units. One for the older children's study room and one for the kitchen. Well, she was speechless and very humble. She couldn't quite understand why we and people from Europe would want to donate to the home. It is a state run home with very little funding and we explained that was exactly the reason we wanted to help the children as they have so little. I then asked if they needed any school books or clothing. Books they didn't need but clothing and shoes they most definitely did but she almost seemed embarrassed to accept. Nick explained that the Corfu villages books were still selling and they must take advantage of the donations while the money is there as it won't last forever and so we agreed to work out a plan so they can take the children shopping and I will pick up the bill. A great meeting was had and it was good to know that the children and staff were happy. As we left Nick said I was "Saint Stefanos" and just said that whenever I walk out of the home I feel blessed to have been able to help such a worthy cause.

On Thursday we were invited to Ipsos by Simon Badderley to sail aboard his 29 foot yacht to Lazeretto Island (Pirate Island) in the words of his grandson. There wasn't much wind so we sailed at a leisurely 6 knots and reached the Island after about an hour. We took it in turns steering the boat until we were about to dock and Simon and his friend, Dave the captain took over. If you know the history of Lazaretto you will know it is still a very sad and poignant place and if you don't know then take a look online. As you walk up the short hill you are greeted by some 160 graves on both sides of the track. A small church appears in front and is being renovated but inside we found the icons were beyond repair. On the left hand side of the clearing is a large building which is being renovated and will be a museum. As we looked back we could see the wall of an old building with a cenotaph and a few graves with wreaths dried out from the sun. As we cruised back we reflected on Corfu's turbulent history as we ate spanakopita and pork pie with cheese supplied by Dave.

When we got back on land we popped in to see Sally Tinkler at Sally's bar. She had some money for me from the sale of the books but I told her to keep it and give it to the man who had Leukaemia for which she was raising money for. We had a couple of drinks and then headed to Dassia to see an old Greek friend of 27 years who owns the Red penguin bar. Spiros and Dina had prepared a room for us to stay the night and we had a drink with him and two of his regular customers Brenda and John who we know from Facebook. A quick shower and then off on the scooter up north to see another old friend Aleko Damaskinos at the kafenion in Nissaki where we discussed the possibility of translating the Corfu villages book into Greek. Then it was back down to Barbati to drop off two signed copies of the Corfu villages books at a taverna there and then downhill to Sally's bar for the Hungarian

Beatles tribute band. I had arranged a meeting with the angel himself, Martin Brindley and with a table for five we accompanied by Ken Harrup and his lovely wife. I donated the money from the two books I had just sold to Sally's cause and gave her some more books to sell and said she could also donate this money too. Ken the gave me 50 euros from the winner of the 100 club and asked if it could be donated to the children's home as this was the wish of the benefactor. After a couple of hours we rode back to the Red Penguin for a few late drinks and a catch up with Spiros. What a busy day!

On Friday Nick and I went to the Kotsovolos electrical shop to buy the air conditioning units. Christos was there who served us last time so we bought the best units with dual air conditioning and a heater for the winter. The price with fitting came to 1200 euros and Christos gave us 10% discount bless him.

Now it was time for a trip to some beaches. The next day the weather looked a bit grey so Ann and I headed down to the beaches of Agios Mattheos. We had a stroll around Paramonas and Skala and then had lunch at Prasoudi. I love the taverna there and we spent a couple of hours just gazing out to the sea at the small rocks off the shore and walked barefoot on the golden sand. The weather had improved as soon as we reached Prasoudi and the sun continued to shine all day. We lazed around for the last two days before heading back to

England with the thought that although we had only had a one week holiday it had been a very enjoyable one.

April 2017 and we arrived late on Saturday night as usual and was picked up by Nick and as is customary I dropped my bag at the apartment and we headed for the village to see some friends and have a few beers. Then a few more beers as the bar was very busy with live music and lots of people. On Sunday morning another friend Nick Pagiatis came round to our place for breakfast as my wife, who was there the week before with her friends had bought me a welcome pack of bacon, eggs, milk and orange juice. But, we decided to head for Alexandros taverna and have an English breakfast there as I had a late night and didn't fancy cooking. We had a lazy day scootering around and unexpectedly met a Danish man named Kim Jaque in Vatos who I had arranged to meet the next day. Kim took us to meet Maria aged 83 and her husband Spiros aged 89 who were the owners of the Spiros 97 taverna and minimarket which they had opened and have run for 60 years.

On Monday we went back to Vatos to meet a Kim for breakfast. Kim told me all about the hippy days when the Island was first colonised by the long haired youngsters from Europe, Scandinavia, America and Australia. He had many old photographs and some great stories. My breakfast of a special omelette was cooked by a German friend, Dagmar Jahn and set me up for the walk that our guide Kim was to take us on.

Up, up and up we went, through the olive groves to the gateway to the Agios Georgios mountain where at last we could descend and through the deserted village of Trialos. A flat walk around the headland bought us to a house full of orange and lemon trees. We were greeted with a tsipouro and water and I sat for a while gazing at the different herbs and fruit that were all around us. Anise (aniseed) thyme, rosemary, oregano, potatoes, tomato plants and flowers too. We then headed to the Myrtiotissa monastery. Then down, down, down to Myrtiotissa beach which only meant one thing. We had a long walk back up to the main road. Kim took us to the monastery to meet Father Daniel but it was mid afternoon when we arrived and we think he was either having a siesta or had gone out. Kim knew where the key to the chapel was and we looked inside at the beautiful icons. Father Daniel lives there alone and his vocation is to reintroduce the flora and fauna to the grounds. We took a pit stop at Elia taverna near the top where we were given a bottle of water by the owners as the taverna was not open yet and then a short walk through the woodland bought us to the Kelia lake and the wildlife. After a six or seven kilometre walk which seemed to be mainly uphill, it was time for a beer and some lunch.

On Tuesday I headed for my meeting with Bob Bakker from the Netherlands.

Bob has been a very generous with his donations to the Children's home and we went for lunch at Rouvas by the market in Corfu town. We then went to the home and I showed Bob the bicycles and air conditioning units I had bought for them. Bob was a bit shocked at the disrepair and conditions of the house and said that when he got back to Holland he would see if there was anything else he could do to help.

I was back in town on Wednesday to meet with Sally and Clive Harmsworth who provide the mobility scooters and aids to tourists in the north of Corfu and I had invited them to accompany me on my meeting with Andreas Skoupouros, the president of the Disabled society. The meeting went well and later that night I spoke to the

Mayor of Pelekas, Alekos Martinez about placing a floating disabled wheelchair for Glyfada beach which Andreas had agreed to supply free of charge. Andreas is a fantastic young guy who is disabled himself and is achieving great things on the Island. He also answered a lot of questions that Sally and Clive wanted to know about how hotels and apartments could improve facilities for disabled people who visit Corfu.

Thursday was supposed to be a trip to the waterfalls of Nimfes and a coffee with Valerie Morrow but with no rain for a few weeks the waterfall was dry so Nick and I headed to the "Friends of Corfu" charity bake off event where we met many people who support the poor and needy. I gave Martin Brindley 200 euros for a cooker he had bought for the psychiatric home and we chatted with everyone and ate homemade pork pie and had a beer. Next stop was the Red Penguin for breakfast with my old friend of 30 years, Spiros. But, it hadn't opened for the season yet so we carried on to Sally's in Ipsos but that too was closed. I said let's go for a swim at Nissaki and have lunch at Mitsos taverna as by now we were starving. When we got there it was closed. I saw the owner Katerina on the beach so had a quick chat and we decided to head back down to Barbati and stop at the first taverna that was open on the main road. We had a seafood platter with octopus, calamari, fish, fried aubergines, courgettes and a large beer.

On Friday we rode up to Doukades to pick up the book "A year on a Greek Island" by Maddie Grigg (Margery Hookings) A signed copy had been there waiting for me for over a year and after an initial panic in the village the postman was located and the book was retrieved from his house. Then it was the long ride up the northwest coast to meet Mandy and Terry Lockett. They have rebuilt a house opposite a chapel in Prinilas and the views are stunning. We had coffee and went down the road to meet Dimitris (Jimmy) and Eleni at the famous 007 James Bond café at Pagi. They had laid on a meze lunch and we talked about the café, the Corfu villages book and the charities but I was humbled by his generosity and genuine interest. He asked me if I would bring some more books when I next visited as he liked to give them to his favourite customers. We then drove to the Porto Timoni headland but decided not to make the walk down to the beach as it was a good thirty minutes walk from the top and time was getting on.

Saturday was my last day and I spent a few hours cleaning the apartment and packing my bag. I went up to Pelekas to say my goodbyes and had lunch with my adopted family, George and Rodula Kontis from the Hawaii pool bar. Yes, it was closed, but not for me. We ate homemade chicken soup with vegetables and for me it was the best meal of the week. After kisses and the promise to come back soon I went back to the apartment, put the scooter to bed and waited for my lift to the airport from Nick. I poured a glass of red wine and went outside to sit on the patio looking over the countryside to the sea, Corfu town and the Greek mainland. The view is magnificent and I never tire of the constant change in the sky whether there are clouds, sun or rain. The colours are vivid and being in an elevated position are clear and uninterrupted. Yellow is the striking colour as the sun rises in the morning. The blue of the sky and the green of the olive landscape dominate the daytime. Orange and reds dance around as the sun goes down on another perfect day on Corfu. I can see why the Cofiots love their Island and also why tourists like us want to live there.

My second trip to Corfu was a short five day holiday in June with some friends.

Five of us on a "Lads" holiday with a strict rules for me to get back to being a tourist for just once and resume my charity work when I go back for nine days in September. This was quite difficult for me as so many of my holidays in the past few years has had a plan that has included the Corfu charities.

We arrived in the afternoon for a change as we flew from our nearest airport with Ryanair from Birmingham. A taxi to Wolverhampton station and a half an hour train ride to the airport starting out at 05.00 am. I checked in three of us at the same time early on the check in day hoping that we would all sit together. I had checked to see the availability of three seats together and there were plenty. I clicked the check in now button and received my seat numbers. 10B, 11F and 14B. Then I got a message "Would you like to sit together?" I checked the price of the seats either side of me and they were £10 extra each. Ryanair had changed their policy which was to split every party up and even couples who don't buy a seat. When we all got on the plane we swapped seats with other people so it was nice to beat the system for once.

I had ordered scooters for everyone in Pelekas already but at our apartment my bike wouldn't start. So I hitched a lift with Bob to Corfu town to buy a new battery and a spark plug. The shops were closed so we had a couple of beers in San Rocco, took in the sunset on Kontogialos beach and had souvlaki in Pelekas. We managed to catch up with friends in the local bars and an early night. 1.00am is early or us but it had been an early start and we wanted to get up early for a change.

On this break we had decided that we were going to do something different and go to places we hadn't been to before so day two we were heading for Messonghi for a swim and a fish lunch on the beach at Meraki taverna. A local friend had fixed my scooter as the new battery and spark plug had not quite worked as there was a perished pipe so all was well. I had dreamt about this meal through the winter months and my friend Nick picked us up from the village drove us down in his car. Two of the lads did different things in the day and we would meet up in the evenings so we were the three musketeers. The meal was everything I had dreamt of as Nick ordered a sea bream, gavros, sardines, grilled calamari, fried calamari and Greek salads for four. The fish had been delivered that day by Nick's brother Babbis.

Day three and we rode over to Corfu town to get the boat to Vidos Island. It is a lovely Island with a Serbian history, a small beach, many pine trees with rabbits and pheasants running free. It was very tranquil there and they played ambient music to suit the surroundings in the famous and only Menios taverna. I met the manager we talked about Corfu and the Corfu villages book and he said that he was involved with many businesses on the Island and if I wanted to live on Corfu he would find me a job.

After a few hours we took the boat back as the evening drew near and the sun hit Corfu town in front of us. We were hungry now and went to "Nino's" in town for dinner. This taverna has the food already cooked and you choose from the many stainless steel trays laid out at the counter. As we rode back to Pelekas we took the steep right hand bend opposite the Triklino wine estate. The bend is quite sharp and Dave approached it too fast. He was heading for the opposite side of the road and applied the brakes but it was too late. The bike slid from underneath him and he went sliding across the road wearing a pair of shorts, a tee shirt and no helmet. I jumped off my scooter and quickly ran over to pick him up and guide him to the side of the road. The cars on the opposite side of the road had luckily seen what was before them and had stopped and asked us if we needed any help. Dave said that he was OK and I suggested that we go to the Hawaii pool bar to see what injuries he had. When we arrived I told Dave to go with me straight away to the toilet washroom where I could take a look at his cuts and bruises and wash them. After his cuts were washed he lay down on a sun bed and I asked Rodula for the Greek equivalent of the brown coloured and very painful Iodine. She had some in the house and I dabbed the many cuts that Dave had and to my surprise it didn't sting. He had cuts and scrapes all over his right side on his toes, shin, thigh and arm. This didn't seam to bother him too much as we have played football together for many years and had always had cuts and bruises but he said his shoulder was painful a this took the brunt of the fall as he hit the ground. When we got back to the UK Dave went to the hospital for a x-ray as he was still in pain, there was nothing broken but he had torn ligaments in his shoulder. I always wear jeans, a jacket and a helmet when I venture out of the village so be warned. After dinner and a few beers Bob took Dave home and later we decided to have another early night at 02.00am.

The next day was our last full day so I had arranged for us to have a day on the west coast with a Greek friend who has a speedboat. We had a German/English breakfast in Kelia near Vatos and met on Pelekas beach at midday. With supplies on board (Wine, beer and sandwiches) we headed north and after visiting some blue caves we dropped anchor for a swim and a picnic at Yiali beach which you can only access with a boat. After lunch we went back down south and passed Ermones, Mirtiotissa, Glyfada, Kontagiaolos and Yialiskai. Another place on my wish list was the small Island of the Panagia Kyra Dikaia. 164 steps uphill to the small church at the top with an older church adjacent. We saw three hare's and there are hundreds of seagulls who nest on the rock. There is a pilgrimage from Pelekas once a year to celebrate the saints day the "Lady of Justice." We had a meze and wine at the lovely Yialikari fish taverna on the way back and lessons in Ancient Greek.

We arrived on Corfu late on Monday 11th September and as usual we dropped the bags at our apartment and headed for the village. I reached into my bag for my wallet but it wasn't there? We searched around and realised I must have left it on the plane as that was the last time I had used it. Luckily I had taken 300 euros out of the wallet shortly before we landed, but, I still had two debit cards, 130 euros, a £20 note and photos of our children in there. We went up to Pelekas where I cancelled the two debit cards and settled down for a drink with friends and suggested we go to the airport when we were in town and see if the wallet had been handed in.

In the morning I rolled my scooter out from its resting place and was looking forward to a quick start as in June I had bought a new battery and spark plug but no such luck. I battled for half an hour without success using the electric start and the kick starter. Today was a free day before we headed off to the mainland to visit the resort of Parga on the ferry and on the scooter. I phoned a Greek friend who is a mechanic and lives a short distance down the road but he was in Germany. We walked to the village to ask if anyone else could help but to no avail. I pushed the scooter down the path to our neighbours house and left the keys and a note to say if they could arrange to fix the scooter I would be back in three days after our mini holiday.

Day three and we caught the bus to Corfu town (2.70€) and walked down to the old port. We had a wait of an hour before the next ferry so had tiropita and a coffee for breakfast. The ferry took around 1 hour 50 minutes to Igoumenitsa (22€) and arrived at 15.00pm. There are two buses a day from the port to Parga. One at 07.30am and one at 13.30pm. So we negotiated a taxi (60 euros) down to a fare of 50 euros for the journey. The taxi only took 35 minutes in the Mercedes along the new roads built for the Greek Olympic games, mind you Gregorios was driving at 140 km/p/hour. We arrived at Marina's rooms which is next door to the Kastro at the top of the town with the houses tumbling down to the harbour and the sea. The room was superb and the view from the bedroom window and the balcony was spectacular. To the right was the impressive Kastro built in 1380. Straight ahead was the sea and the beautiful Island of Saint Mary and to the left was the town and the day tripper boats and the harbour tavernas. There have been many changes to Parga since we last visited 15 years ago but mostly good and we had a brilliant mini break visiting places old and new and even managed to see old friends who made a big Greek welcome as always.

We caught the bus from Parga (6.70 euros) to the port and took a faster ferry to Corfu this time and when we arrived it felt like we were coming home and that we had been away for ages. We went up to the village for dinner and had an early night

(01.00am) as we wanted to be up early the next day to fix the scooter.

The next morning I awoke at just after 07.00am and decided to get up as I wanted to take some sunrise photos. Our apartment is above sea level and has views over the valley to Corfu town on the right, Afra to the sea and to the left Mount Pantokrator. In the distance are the Albanian and Greek mountain ranges. I opened the shutters and stood on the balcony to find the most amazing view. Before me lay a blanket of mist covering the valley and the hues of blue, pink, yellow and orange as the sun began to show its bright yellow crown.

Lunch would be down at Kontogialos beach (Pelekas) with a table for ten. My Greek friend's family were together on

Corfu. Nick and his friend Eleni. Guy and Jessica from the UK. Pavlos and Chloe and their little ones Leo and Melina Sofia from Evropouli. I walked down to see my neighbours to see if they had any luck starting my scooter. Xristos and Stamatis had fixed it for no charge. Now we could get around and go wherever we wanted, whenever we wanted for the rest of the holiday.

A few lazy days and nights followed until it was time to go to the electrical shop Kotsovolos to buy the final air conditioning unit for the children's home in Analypsis, Corfu town. This unit was for the children's study room where it was very warm in the summer and as you may know the children in Greece have a lot of homework. It would cool the room in the summer and heat the room in the Winter. The price was 625 eours with 25% off and I negotiated a free delivery and fitting worth 80 euros. The two units that we bought in April had been fitted in the kitchen so they still needed one for the study.

The next day we decided to have a ride out. We rode to Paleokastritsa and stopped just short at the rocky bay of La Grotta. This is a very trendy Mediterranean bar with tables and chairs set on different levels overlooking the small rocky bay. It's a mainly young crowd listening to chill out music, drinking frappe and jumping from the rocks or diving from the springboard into the turquoise water below. I jumped in from the rocks with my new face mask and snorkel and swam around for a while gazing t the hundreds of fish of all sizes and colours.

I have been to many village festivals or Panigiri's over the years but last years in Pelekas was one to remember. The main festival is on 23rd August at the Theotokos Odigitria church in honour of the virgin Mary. This is held in the main square and has a live Greek band, food stalls and Greek dancing and is attended by over 1,000 locals and tourists. At the upper of the village is the second church of Saint Nikolaos. This panigiri takes place in May and is a much smaller affair with a local band, no stalls and around 30 locals and a few tourists. I first went to this one when we bought our property ten years ago.

Last year I had a two week break on my own as my wife Ann doesn't have as many holiday days as I do. The first week was spent meeting with different people for the Corfu charities and the second week two friends Bob and Dave were due out for five days. The previous October a Greek friend had showed me a video of a Zembetiko dance that I said was my favourite. I said that I would dance this solo at the next panigiri in Pelekas. This friend is Dimitris the Greek dancer from Pelekas and he is well known on the Island as he and his two nephews are young and are members of the Greek dance group. Dimi told me to practice over the winter months and I could dance at the May panigiri but with one word of advice…. "You have to feel the music file, it is not just about the moves"!

So, as the night arrived imagine my surprise when we went up to the village to find a Danish rock band, a children's dance school, toy and souvlaki stall and over two hundred people! It was about 10.00 pm and we had eaten our meal and took a seat in a bar opposite the church to watch the children dance and then band came on and did their first set until 11.00 pm. Then the Greek music started and my friends the Greek dancers Dimi, Spiros and Kostas danced and then involved everyone in the village dances. At 12.00 I heard the word Paragalya which means "This dance for me" In Greece when you ask for a solo dance, no one else can dance as a matter of respect for the person who wants to show his feelings for a dance with a deep feeling for him. The lads approached me and said your turn to dance file mou...Ok, I said, I will just finish this beer and have a cigarette. No they said, Steve you are on now! I looked up from rolling my cigarette to see an empty square. Everyone had stopped dancing and were waiting for me as the introduction to the song started. I walked into the middle of the plateia followed by Bob and Dave and gave them 50 white napkins each. I told them to kneel down and clap to the beat when I did and throw the napkins at my feet 10 at a time during the dance. I walked around and started to clap to the 100 audience that surrounded me. I took off my jacket and threw it to the people in front and my arms went up. I love this song and any nerves soon disappeared as I went into a trance and all the moves I had learned became natural. Dimi was right, if you feel the music the audience know and they respond accordingly. I finished the dance with a kick lifting the napkins off the floor and into the air and a jump landing on one knee with arms outstretched. Well, the response was amazing. A round of applause which seemed to last a lifetime. Then hours of congratulations from everyone. The leader of the children's group is one of the best female dancers on Corfu came over and said. "You felt it Steve, Bravo!" which made me very proud. Dimi came over and said, "A few too many moves but you felt the music and you are now the Pelekas Magas! The Magas is the most respected person in the village! Tears came to my eyes...I couldn't hold back the emotion anymore. The experience had humbled me. To be judged and accepted by these wonderful people from my village is truly an honour....But, this is Corfu and its people...

Well, I have had many great nights out on Corfu but one night turned out to be a cracker!

I was in Corfu town one day with Peter and Ciska our Dutch neighbours from Pelekas. We had to pay some bills and decide to have a drink and a meze in San Rocco while we waited an hour for the bus back to Pelekas. We sat down at a table outside and ordered our drinks. The meze was free and it was a big plate with Greek potatoes, Corfu sausage, cheese pies, ham and cheese, very nice! I looked up and noticed on the wall a poster for a famous pop singer who was to appear on Corfu. I said to my friends, Look! "Tamta" is playing on Corfu...Tonight! Shall we go? Yes, they said. We paid the bill and I asked the waiter about the gig. He said, Dou you know Tamta? Yes, I said, I listen to Greek pop music in England! He laughed and said I would be luck to get a ticket as she was so popular now but you can have the posters I have and get them signed if you are lucky? Xa xa!

So, we headed back to Pelekas and decided to get ready early and make our way back to the Mercedes club on the port road near to Mandouki. It was 7.30pm when we arrived and and had plenty of time to have dinner in the taverna nearby. We told the owners where we were going and they said the club didn't open until 10.30 pm! So we had a few beers with the locals and asked if we could smoke? Yes they said but you have to move to the next table as this was the smoking area, Ha ha!

At 10.30 we walked down the road and we were the first ones there? The doormen were there and we asked what time the club opened. 11.00 they said. So, over the next half an hour we talked to the head doorman and he asked us why we were there as the crowd expected tonight would be young Greeks. I told him that Tamta was my favourite singer and I had come all the way from England to see her and my friends had also come from Holland. His name was Alex, he was about 6ft 2" good looking and well built. We got on really well and when he knew we had properties in Pelekas advised us to take a table inside as this would be the best view. 100 euros for a table with a bottle of Vodka and coke with strawberries. Was he about to rip us off? By now there was a big crowd outside trying to push their way in. Alex took us inside and said to the cashier, these are my friends from Pelekas and they want the best table. We paid and went inside the club. We were shown to a table right next to the stage and were served with our drinks. Tamta came on at 12.00 and sang for an hour and a half and it was great. When she left the stage I said to my Peter and Ciska. Would you like to meet Tamta? How the hell are we going to do that Steve? Watch this I said...

I found Alex and reminded him how far we had come to see Tamta and that I listened to Corfu pop fm every night, who were the sponsors, and that we wanted to meet her. Alex looked at me as if to say it was impossible but went backstage to ask her. After a few minutes he came back and said, Endaxi file mou, pame! (Ok my friend, let's go! Tamta was lovely. She made a fuss and she signed the posters I had with me. Pop fm were great too, what a night.

We ordered a taxi as it was now 4.00 am. We thanked and said goodbye to Alex and headed home. By this time it was getting light. The taxi driver asked us if we wanted to see a lake on the way home? Ok we said. A lake in the middle of the Island, is he serious? Yes he was, but that is another story.

I love many beaches on Corfu but one of my favourite beaches is Pelekas beach. Called Kontogialos in Greek or Steno by the locals. We had spent several holidays on Corfu, Paxos and Parga on the mainland before buying our place in Pelekas village. The first time I went to the beach was with my brother in law. We had gone to Pelekas for a week in May to see how the apartment was progressing as it was being renovated after the building had been empty for 10 years. Pelekas lies on the central west coast some 300 metres above sea level. We decided to walk down and take in the views as we descended. It took around 20 minutes to reach the beach and was very steep in places. Our calves were a bit stiff and wearing flip flops was definitely a bad idea. It was the first week of the season so we expected it to be quiet and it was only 11.00 am as we turned the last corner and viewed the beach for the first time. Wow! A kilometre wide beach of golden sand with no one on it! We lay down and took in the early sunshine as the weather in England had been cold and wet. We ran into the sea to cool off and dived into the crashing waves as the wind blew in. Out of breath we walked over to the taverna Tassos in the middle of the beach. The taverna was owned by an older couple in their late seventies. They spoke very little English so it gave me a chance to use my Greek to order lunch and to tell them why we were here. It was an old fashioned place where the locals went and very different from the more up to date restaurants either side. We had a lovely lunch of meze and beer and taking in the panoramic view of the sea. But, it was mid afternoon and time to make our accent back to the village for a siesta. Half an hour later and after several stops in the hot afternoon sun we finally reached the top. It was like climbing Mount Everest! Never again would I walk to the beach and back. In high summer there is a small village bus that takes people down and back up but it depends on local funding and the generosity of one of the local bus drivers. I would hire a car or a scooter for a few days on future holidays to ferry the family down for the day and a few years ago bought a scooter for me and Ann now the children are older and doing their own thing.

Chapter 8. Corfu characters.

The first character I met on Corfu was the owner of the "Limeri taverna" in Kato Korakiana, he was the first Greek person that I met as we ate there on our first ever night on Corfu. He was a big man, quite tall but deceiving as he was broad and had a big frame. He had black curly hair and a huge traditional Greek moustache. We met in 1987. He had a nice manner. He was warm and patient as I read the menu out to my friend in Greek and English. We ordered in Greek and he smiled and asked where we were from. We told him that it was our first time in Corfu and he welcomed us. There was a guitar on the wall but it must have been there a long time as it wasn't playable. There were pictures on the wall of Old Corfu and some of what I presume were his family. The minor bird nearby was talking away and the music was nice, Rembetika I think. The meal was lovely. In those days I was a finicky eater so the Chicken breast with Greek salad and a few chips were fine. The Chicken was cooked on the grill and was so soft and tender, it was delicious. I had never had a meat so tasty. The girls that served us didn't speak much English so we improvised in "Gringlish" my favourite language and the service was excellent. It is still one of my favourite tavernas even now. We still go back to visit when we can or when we are over Dassia way. I remember when we sat down for the first time there. There were a few older English, German and Dutch couples already seated there. It seemed like they were watching our every move and listening to everything we said but...we were young and loud then.

Aleko Damaskinos.

Aleko lives in a hamlet above Barbati on the main road by the resort and grew up in Kapadistriou street in Corfu town. He is a diminutive build with thick black/grey hair and more recently a long grey beard. He is a professor of Mathematics and attended the Edinburgh university in Scotland. He wears a simple cotton shirt and a pair of smart trousers and although he is short he has a presence. He is extremely intelligent and is very well respected on Corfu as he has a vast knowledge of the Island and the flora and fauna. He told me that he has bread and olive oil for breakfast every day and thinks this is the recipe for long life. It is a privilege for me to know him and he was kind enough to write a passage on the history of two of the villages of the book. I remember going to the Vitamins taverna one night with him and his friend Chris Holmes, who's mother had lived above Gouvia for many years. We were a party of ten people and ordered food fit for a King. Aleko, Chris and I had some food but were more interested in telling old stories, drinking beer and smoking cigarette's. Aleko's sister is linguist and has translated the first eBook on the Corfu central region into Greek but I had the time to release it yet.

Lavinia Psarras.

I met Lavinia on Facebook many years ago and we have been friends ever since. She has some great stories about Corfu in the sixties when she went to live in Corfu town with her Corfiot husband who was a top surgeon on the Island. She also lived for a time in Kapodistriou street where the Rex and Aegli tavernas vie to be the oldest in town and both boast to be the first in 1932. She remembers Aleko and his family living there too. Lavinia is quite posh but is very down to earth. She is a fighter and a survivalist as her husband died at an early age and she was left in the house behind Kinopiastes to bring up two small children. Everyone knows her in the village and she speaks excellent Greek which gives her a lot of respect. She told me a story once when there was a very ill man in Kasioppi and they had to go up there to give him some treatment. The road up the coast from Ipsos was a dirt track then and when they got there they had to show their passports to enter the village. She is quite tall with long hair and has the ability to talk with anyone from whatever background. Maybe that's because of the jobs she has had with the British government in her younger days and the extravagant lifestyle she enjoyed sitting next to Kings and Princes at official parties. Once, she took me down to Boukari on the south east coast for a lunch of baby calamari and Greek salad, it was delicious and she introduced me to the beauties of the south.

Andreas Skoupouras.

Andreas works for the Corfu council and is the new kid on the block. He is a young man and is tenacious and very focussed on the issues of the disabilities faced by people on Corfu and Greece. He is disabled himself and therefore fully understands the problems faced by others in the same situation as he has experienced life in a wheelchair and has used walking sticks himself from a young age. He is building ramps where the only access to buildings were steps and is introducing wider and disabled parking bays in Corfu town. He is now vice mayor and speaks at seminars around Greece many of which are televised. I was impressed with his ideas and he is responsible for the floating wheelchairs that are now on many beaches on Corfu. He told me that when he was young his father had to pick him up and take down to the sea where he would hold him in the water. Now the new floating wheelchairs will give all the disabled people of all ages on the Island the chance to bathe in the sea.

Martin & Wendy Brindley.

If they call me Agios Stefanos (Saint Steve) then Martin Brindley has to be the Archangel Gabriel and Wendy, Mother Theresa. Martin and his wife Wendy have retired and have a house on Corfu. After working in Leeds for many years and being involved in helping local charities they decided to continue their good work for the less fortunate people on Corfu. After starting the "Friends of Corfu" group they are now more or less working full time for the Corfu charities and I salute them for their compassionate work on the ground. They are naturally happy people and it is an honour to know them both.

Spiros (Giros) Grannas.

My best friend on Corfu is Spiros from the souvlaki shop in Pelekas. He has retired now and is recovering from an operation he had on his back last year. Gossip in the village said that he would never walk again but I went to visit him at his house in the village this summer and he is getting better day by day. He is the older Greek brother I never had and he is a treasure. His pride and joy is his chocolate brown 1970's Ford Cortina mark 4. He has a framed photograph of me and my brother in law, Kenny, posing either side of the car like Dennis Waterman and John Thaw from the seventies hit series of "The

Sweeney". He has a retro Adidas tracksuit in navy blue with white stripes and a red trim and I have been trying to buy the top off him for ten years to no avail. He wears a baseball cap and has a white goatee beard but now he has retired is more often seen in a smart shirt. He spent many years in Cardiff when he was younger but funnily enough didn't inherit the Welsh accent.

Kevin Baker.

Kevin was a lovely man in his forties and always looked for the positives about Corfu and that is probably why we got on so well. He had a house in a village near Acharavi and at one time had owned a bar. He was interested in social media and when he asked me if he could come down to Pelekas to interview me about the Corfu villages book I was a bit nervous. But he was very professional and made me feel at ease. I enjoyed the interview and I think that it was because of the way Kevin asked the questions. He was genuinely interested in what I was doing to help the community and released a video of the interview on YouTube again free of charge. It is with great regret that Kevin passed away last year after a short illness. They say only the good die young and he will be sorely missed.

Chapter 9. Village Life.

Although we had now visited Corfu for many summers we didn't know a lot about the villages. Of course we had driven through many of them when we had hired a car and gone on day trips to other resorts. But the village life was somewhat of a mystery to us but now we had bought the apartment in Pelekas this was about to change. My brother in law and I had been to the tavernas and bars in the village when we had been the year before but the next family holiday would be a totally different experience as Ann, Eva and Bobby had never had a village holiday.

We bought our flight tickets online several months before we were due to fly out as the budget airlines prices go up the nearer you get to the date of flying. This is apparent to independent travellers now but in 2008 it was new to us. I had met the local taxi driver in the village and there he was waiting at the arrivals gate as we walked out. What a refreshing change it was to be greeted by a friendly taxi driver and to be driven the twelve kilometres to the apartment in a brand new Mercedes than to be queuing to catch the coach to a resort with all the drop offs. Things got even better when we reached our destination after twenty minutes and the driver Dimitris helped us with the suitcases up the hill to our new home. It was dark when we arrived and when I opened the front door I reached behind to turn the electric on. The lights came on and I walked in followed by the family and stood back to gauge their reaction to their now well appointed second home. Wow! Was the reaction as they gazed around and looked in the cupboards, the drawers, the bathroom and the kitchen. I must admit it did look good and I thank Kenny for his help the year previous. Yes, we had partied on the night time but we had worked hard in the daytime to get the apartment fit for a family holiday and to make it look more like a home than a rented accommodation. The family were pleased and so was I, this was a new type of holiday that we would enjoy for many years to come and it would also change the way we viewed Corfu completely.

We had bought a few things with us for our breakfast as we were not quite sure what the local minimarket had to offer in way of food. So, we delved into the hand luggage for tea bags, coffee and sugar. I had bought some English bacon and a block of mature English cheese so at least we could have something to eat and drink before we headed up to the village to see what they had.

There were several walks up to Pelekas from the apartment. There was the back way up the hill which would take you through the olive groves. You walk up past the "Papas with the goats" house until you reach the first house of the village. This is Papas number two in the village and he assists the main Papas of the area with his duties. I have never met him personally but you will recognise him instantly if he out and about as he drives a long forked three wheeled farmers tractor everywhere he goes. You pass Dimitris (Mitsos) house and walk to the first of two really steep alleyways which will eventually bring you to the centre of the village by the main church of Theotokos Odigitria. This is the church where the Papas of the Paralion area of Corfu presides.

Papa Labis is his name and he is a very well respected and kind man who I think one day is destined for higher office. You can do this walk in under ten minutes so it is the quickest route, but you will need a few stops to take a breather as it is very steep.

The second and most familiar way to the village is to simply walk up the main Pelekas road which is a couple hundred metres at a steady incline, bear right when you reach the beach road, past the cemetery on your left and walk up to the centre. This walk will take twenty minutes. The third and favoured walk of our family and friends is to walk up the main road for one hundred metres and take a shortcut through "Cat alley" and up to the village with just two steep alleys up to the church. This walk takes around fifteen minutes and we use this way most of the time because we can't always use the olive grove path as it is overgrown or wet in the early season. The walk to the village is a trek but one thing is for sure, it is a hell of a lot easier walking down hill on the way home after a good night out.

There are many tavernas and bars in Pelekas which is unusual for a village on Corfu but that is due to the many returning visitors from the hippy days of the 70's and 80's. That is great for us as it resembles a resort with a village feel on a hill so we get the best of both worlds.

We had some breakfast and chose the olive grove way up to the village. I was eager to show the family around so we started with the first taverna as you enter Pelekas which is called "Roula's" Roula is a very nice lady in her fifties. She is slim with dark hair and has a welcoming smile. Her husband is Michalis and he is a great souvlaki chef. Opposite the taverna is an open loading truck. Mikey as I call him cooks kontasouvli, pork rollo and lamb at Easter (Paska) on the back of the truck using large souvlaki spits which are seated across from one side to the other. The coals are lit underneath on the base of the flat bed container. This is a great idea because when you enter the village you get the beautiful smell of meat cooking drifting down the street and it is difficult to walk past. A master stroke from Mikey I think as although the taverna is small it is always busy. We have eaten there many times and the reason I like it is the fact that when you order a Greek meal like lamb chops it is often served with chips only? At Roula's she will serve you with meat, Greek potatoes, (my favourite) and any vegetable that she has from her garden. It could be green beans, carrots or broccoli but I like that touch. Maybe I should teach them how to make gravy?

Mikey is a character, he is quite short and rounded with grey thinning hair and always has a red face because of cooking in front of the grill. He wears a similar shirt every night and is brighter than you think. He makes me laugh when he walks into the quite trendy Zanzibar in the square when it is packed and he has just finished work around twelve o'clock. The bar is filled with people of all ages from all over Europe who speak mainly in English and Mikey will walk in and take his usual chair at the bar for his well earned drink. He doesn't look or talk to anyone and is just oblivious to what is happening around him. For him this is his village and it doesn't matter who is there as he has always had a drink after work there since it opened in the 70's. When I talk to him in Greek he answers me in English...Nice guy.

As you turn the corner you will enter the beginning of the square. On the left is the souvlaki giros café. The word souvlaki derives from the medieval Greek word "Souvla" which means skewer. This was our first port of call as Kenny and I had eaten here many times the year before and I was keen for the family to meet the owners, Spiros (Gyros) Grana, his wife Maria and their daughter Stefania. Of all the people that I had met previously Spiros was the one I connected with the most. He was five feet eight inches tall, the same as me. He was balding but I didn't know this until the following year as he wore a navy blue baseball cap which he rarely took off. He had a white goatee beard, had an insatiable smile and wore a blue retro style Adidas tracksuit. His English was very good as he had lived in Cardiff for twenty years in his twenties but now he had come back to his birthplace to run a family business. I called him "Pateras" (Father) because he looked like my dad and had many of the mesmerisms that my Father had which I found endearing. He never questioned my name for him and it wasn't until many years later that I found out that he was only ten years older than me so I changed his name to "Adelfos mou" (My brother) We ate there on our first night but it was like a kafenion really. Inside there were plastic tables and chairs and Maria would cover the table with a paper map of Corfu, bring a basket of bread and pass me a "Tasaki" (Ashtray) By this time the European no smoking law had been introduced in Greece and was a topic of conversation in every taverna and bar. Spiros smoked and so did I, what was the problem?

"To Steki" was the name above the door. This place was more than that to me over the next few years as we met many Greek people from the village in there and also many German, Dutch and English people who have since become friends. This was Greece at it's best. No airs and graces here, this was a place where the villagers came to eat and talk. There was a constant arrival of scooters and cars who would pull up outside, often in the middle of the road and stop the traffic from passing through. There would be a few blasts on the horn by the people wanting to pass through but again that was no problem as they were served quickly and were soon on their way. I liked the television raised up in the corner of the room. It was a small silver TV that you would have in a bedroom. It would always be on the political channel where the programme would show a split screen of nine politicians shouting at the top of their voices about the state of the economy.

Maria and Stefania would cook the food and Spiros would clean and lay the tables. Then he would bring you the food to your table inside if it was a cool night or to your table over the road in the warm summer nights. They had a dog at the time called "Sunny" He was a very mild tempered dog and looked like a miniature version of a golden Labrador. He must have been hit by a car at some point as he had always walked with a back leg limp as long as I had known him. Sometimes later at night he would amble up the street to the Zanzibar and lay on the welcome mat at the door entrance. He would be waiting for Spiros who would be walking around the bars. We would just step over him and pat or stroke him on the way in. On many occasions he would be laying in the road outside the grill room and cars would have to stop. Spiros would shout at him to move over to the side of the road but always pat him on the head the next time he passed him. He loved that dog and so did everyone in the village.

I had already told Ann that the one shared toilet was not very nice and to this day she has never been in.

As the years went by Spiros and I became very good friends and when he finished work he used to find me in one of the bars and we would go to different places around the village together and have a few beers and talk about England and Greece. I gave him another name after we had a few late nights out and I had to walk him home as he was so drunk. "To Fidi" (The Snake) because he would move like one on the way home! He is a great character and is still a dear friend today.

As you leave the souvlaki place there is a mini market next door so we decided to get some eggs to go with our bacon, some sliced bread for a sandwich and of course some local Kokino krassi (Red wine) I love the local wine as it is probably less than 10% alcohol and a must when you put the kids to bed and have a nightcap on the balcony looking at the millions of stars and gazing through the darkness over the Island to the tiny bright lights to Corfu town and the mainland in the distance.

Next door to the grill house is the Agnes mini market with a choice of fruit and vegetables stacked outside the front window which gives a colourful display to coax in the tourists as they walk by. There is a fridge which contains butter, ham, milk, beer and water. On the one side of the free standing shelving units there are all manner of domestic products like furniture polish, mop and bucket, clothes pegs and cleaning agents for the kitchen and bathroom. On the other side there are cereals, herbs, spices, eggs and bread of all descriptions. The wall on the right hand side of the shop is bursting with tourist bracelets and necklaces, ceramic moulds of brightly coloured Corfu houses, churches and landscapes. All in all there is quite a good choice for a first days shopping for essentials to start a family holiday. Breakfast and lunch could now be made quite cheaply at home giving us the budget to eat out in the tavernas and a few drinks in the bars at evening time.

The next building on the left is the "O Foros" bar. The name means "Forum" or a place to meet and talk and dates back to Roman times. This bar is owned by Alexandros Vergis who's family also own the Alexandros taverna and rooms where we stayed on our first ever visit to the village. Inside here are two large American pool tables, a large television screen which shows the Greek Super league football and basketball games. This area we call kids corner as it mainly attracts all of the young boys from the village. The bar lays straight ahead and to the right there is a cards and back gammon table and a dart board for the older men in the village. Although I have never seen anyone playing darts in there as the card table is stood there against the wall underneath the dart board. I could just imagine throwing darts over the heads at the board whilst four or so villagers sat there playing their games, talking and drinking their coffee or beer. You would not want your dart to come bouncing back in their direction and even if you got all three darts to stick in the board, how would you get them back? This is Greece.

Opposite O Foros is "Agnes taverna" Yes, you guessed it. This family own the mini market too. It is very much a traditional taverna serving all the usual Greek dishes and being in the centre of the village has a very good day time trade as well as at night. Like many tavernas in Greece you can eat outside or inside at Agnes and if you are visiting and feel like spending the night then there are Agnes rooms next door!

As you reach the end of the road by the church there is the Pelekas café on the right and the Zanzibar on the left.

The Pelekas café serves coffee and soft drinks in the morning and beers and alcohol in the afternoon. At night it is one of the busiest bars as the Greeks young and old come from all over the area to drink until the early hours.

On the left is the famous Zanzibar. This was the first bar to open in the village in the 70's and was opened by Jo from Birmingham and her Greek husband Vassilis Koskinas. There son Richard runs the bar now and Kenny and I had some very late nights in there. This bar attracts the returning visitors from the hippy days of the 70's and 80's. Nowadays many of them now bringing their children of all ages with them.

As you turn a sharp left up the hill there is the village bakery. Here they sell all your favourite Greek cakes, baklava, sweets, Pastries and fresh bread which is cooked that morning. Recently they have added some tables and chairs and serve coffee too. It is nice to head up to the village and have a coffee and a pastry here, watch the comings and goings all with the view of the whole street and the beautiful church next door.

The steep walk around the corner brings you to a new shop on the right. They sell a bit of everything in here from a loaf of bread to a pair of ladies tights. Or so Ann told me as I have only ever been in once to buy a tiropita when our fridge was empty and I had to be somewhere fast.

Now, the next business on the left is another famous place. It is "Magissospito" The witches house" Everything and anything you can think of about witches is here and all of the items for sale are hand made. It is a beautiful shop and would not look out of place in a high end street in Corfu town.

Opposite is a tourist shop owned by the lovely Vassilis and his lovely sister Anna. If you want to buy some presents for friends and family or need to stock up on beachwear then this is the place for you. Vassilis is a very knowledgeable about the village and is a member of the Pelekas choir who sing not only on Corfu but around the Greek mainland and Europe. He is in his fifties and a couple of years ago we were invited to his wedding. Anna has two children and is possibly the worse driver I have ever seen in my entire life. I have seen her do a three point turn and I swear it took her over twenty. Pelekas is not the easiest place to turn your car around but why even attempt it when the rush hour traffic is heading back from Glyfada and Mirtiotissa beach.

Pelekas has a lower square and an upper square. I call it Ano Peleka and Kato Peleka much to the amusement of the locals who just call it Pelekas. As you reach the upper square there is the church of Saint Nikolaos which was like so many churches on Corfu built in the 1750's onwards.

On the right hand side is "Jimmy's" taverna and rooms. This is more like a restaurant than a taverna as the food is Greek and Mediterranean. The dishes are more flamboyant with little twists here and there, you could say fancy. Andreas, the son of Jimmy runs it now and he is a very intelligent young man. He is the kind of person who can see the future of tourism on Corfu and has many ideas although he realises the importance of the Greek traditions.

On the left is "Antonis" taverna run by Georgios and his trusted friend and chef Ricardo from Albania. We often go there if we want fresh fish and Rick has never disappointed us. I like to watch him cook the fish over the grill but I don't know how he does it in the heat of summer. It must be over 40 degrees centigrade in the kitchen. On the side wall of the taverna is the most prolific growing jasmine tree. The fragrances from here are beautiful and it doesn't matter how much they cut it back each year it grows back with a vengeance.

Next door to Antonis is the "In Bar" This is a night time bar only and is owned by Aleko and his bilingual wife Roula. This a bar suited to the older crowd although our children love it. Aleko is a short stocky guy in his early fifties with short black and grey hair and a permanent smile. They often have live Greek music here but not the tourist Zorba the Greek. It will be Rembetiko or Zembekiko performed by a three or four piece band. There is a good mix of cultures here. Like the Zanzibar, the people who come here are local Greeks, Dutch, Swedes, Norwegians, Danish and from the UK.

If you follow the road down past the In Bar it will bring you to the "Pink Panther" restaurant. Here there are fantastic views down to Kontogialaos paralia (Pelekas beach). This is the only place I will book a table because of the view but also because of the time we usually eat in the summer which will be around eight o'clock in the evening. As the sun starts its decent it throws up an orange hue to the village trees and houses behind us. I have never seen this anywhere else so far and we and our guests are always amazed by the colours. The family who own the taverna are Greek but have an Italian connection so although they cook Greek food they also have a pizza oven. The food here is very good and my top tip would be to order the lamb chops. Every guest we have taken there have said that the chops are delicious but why do they come with frozen chips? Ask for Greek potatoes, I did.

A little further on and you will arrive at the "Hawaii pool bar" This bar has the best swimming pool in Pelekas and the most delightful hosts. Rodoula and Georgos Kontis used to own a great bar a few years ago next door to the In Bar but decided to move to the edge of the village where they could expand on their own family land. If you want to spend a lazy day by the pool then this is a great place to do it. It is a quiet and peaceful area and is surrounded by lemon trees. They play ambient music in the day time and serve Greek meals as well as bar food such as a club sandwich, an omelette and pizzas.

Take the road back up to the upper village and turn left up the hill to the famous "Kaisers Throne" The first taverna you will come to after passing Jimmy's is "Alexandros taverna" and rooms. This was the first taverna that Kenny and I had eaten in and we still do to this day. This is a bigger family who all work together in the taverna throughout the summer and at weekends in the winter. Front of house is Alex the oldest son. A well built man with a plump face and a rough voice through smoking Greek cigarettes. He always wears a smart shirt and chinos. His hair is tied up in a ponytail and he speaks perfect English. His younger brother Spiros is tall, dark and handsome but does he know it! Stavros is the youngest brother and cooks the meals with his mitera (mother) He is the tallest and is well built but quite slim. He has brown hair and the Vergis smile as they all do. If there is a football game on in town, Stavros and I will go and watch Kerkyra poli (Corfu town) play. Although I don't think he can get his head around the fact that I will go for a beer at half time? The mother and father are lovely and we have many conversations in Greek and English.

The road uphill from Alexandros taverna leads to the "Levant hotel" and "Kaisers throne" The Levant is a hotel for couples as they only have twin or double rooms. There is a nice swimming pool and the gardens are grassed. The restaurant is nicely old fashioned and has paintings of the history of the Kaiser Wilhelm's visits. The decor has light walls and dark furniture. At the centre of the lounge is a roaring fire which is perfect on an early evening at "Paska" (Easter) or a late visit in October. The food is traditional and they hold wedding receptions here. It is a great place to watch the sunset as the courtyard faces the east coast of Corfu where the sun goes down.

Kaisers throne is just opposite the hotel and it is said this is the best view of the Island. To the left you can see over the flat lands of the Ropa valley and to the villages and the hills of the north. Mount Pantokrator and the Albanian mountains. Straight ahead is the whole of the central area of Corfu, Corfu town and the mountains of the Greek mainland. To the right looks towards the Agioi Deka mountain and the villages of Sinarades and Varypatades. If you look to your right you can also see the west coast down as far as Agios Gordios and the village of Pendati in the hills.

The Kaisers throne lookout point was built by Kaiser Wilhelm II of Germany.

In 1907 the Kaiser bought the Achilleion palace at Gastouri from the Empress of Austria, (known as "Sisy") upon her untimely death and resided there in the summer. He would drive to Pelekas and sit at his favourite spot where he could view the fantastic scenery all over the Island. On the grounds of where the Levant hotel is situated now the Kaiser would throw parties and invite his friends from around the Island to enjoy the views and the stunning sunsets.

Pelekas village is perched on top of a hill at around 200 metres above sea level and has a population of around 500 people. From the beach road you can see a few rocks standing alone in the distance. Folklore says that these rocks are the result of a pirate raid. The pirates sailed into the bay of Kontogialos and walked up to the village where there was a wedding taking place. They plundered the village, abducted the bride and carried her off to their ship. The mother of the bride was distraught and shouted out a curse. "I wish my daughter to be turned to stone so that the waves will caress here rather than the hands of the unfaithful" At this the bride, the pirates and the ship were turned to stone.

The name Pelekas comes from the ancient "Pelekis" a type of ancient axe used for cutting wood of stone. The first mention of the village can be found in the historical archives dating back to the 16th century and in the church records in the 17th century.

There are six churches in and around the village and five of them date back to around the 1750's. They all have a yearly festival (panigiri) to honour the saint to who the church is named after, the most famous one which falls on 23rd August attracts over 1,000 people. There is Greek dancing, a live band and of course lamb on the split.

It takes twenty minutes to walk from the village down to Pelekas beach or Kontogialos as the Corfiot's call it. The locals however call it "Stenos" which means a narrow passage as there was no road to the beach before tourism. As you reach half way down you come to a T junction. If you go left it will take you to the large all inclusive hotel with a steep access to the beach. If you walk past the hotel another twenty minute walk will bring you to the small and sandy beach of Yialiskari. There is only one taverna on the beach and many people say it is the best fish taverna on the west coast. I wouldn't disagree and if you eat or drink there you can use the sun beds for free.

Turn right at the junction and you can walk a further ten minutes downhill to the centre of the beach. There is over one kilometre of golden sand with tavernas and bars on either side. The sea is clear and holds a blue flag award for cleanliness. There is a life guard in the high summer, changing rooms and showers to wash away the sand after a day of swimming and laying on the beach. The sea can be rough at times and the waves can get very high especially if there is a strong wind. On a normal day the sea is a delight to swim in and there is nothing I like better than to spend an afternoon there and watch the sun go down.

There is one more road that leads from the village to the beach and is to be found by going through Pelekas and on towards the beaches of Glyfada and Mirtiotissa. As you reach the end of the upper village the road is a further 200 metres down on the left. The road is a more gradual decent this way and the walk will again take a good twenty minutes. The views are spectacular as you walk down with Glyfada on the right and Kontogialos on the left. When you reach the bottom of the road it will bring you to the far right hand side beach. The "Dragon rock" named by me, guards the beach and the small boats which lay protected at the small inlet. Yannis bar stands above the white retaining walls and was the first bar to be built there. It was opened to supply beer for the hippies in the 70's and hasn't changed much at all since. Like so many places on Corfu the bar has its own returning visitors to keep them busy in the summer season. Yiannis is now in his eighties and mainly sits in a chair all day to greet his customers and talk about the "Old days". A couple of years ago he remarried a Bulgarian woman in her forties. His wife and his son had passed away several years ago and I presume he was lonely. Sonia, his new wife has introduced a little food to the menu which consisted of beer, wine, coffee and ice cream. She now cooks pork souvlaki outside on the terrace on a simple outdoor grill. It is very old fashioned but I think their customers prefer it that way. This is village life in Pelekas.

Chapter 10. Reflections.

So, there you have it. A thirty year chronicle of our visits to possibly the best Island on the planet. I had always wanted to write a book about my fondest memories of Corfu and all the adventures I had been on but I had no idea that it would work out the way it did. If someone had told me years ago that I would spend three years travelling around one hundred villages and riding 3,500 kilometres on a scooter that I had bought myself I would have said they were crazy. But after experiencing the hardships of village life and learning about the different worthy causes such as the Red cross, children's homes, the hospital, psychiatric home, disabled society and sick animals, I felt it was my duty to help in some way. The only idea I could come up with was to write about something that I knew very little about and much of it could only be found out by visiting the villages because the information I wanted wasn't published. To write about the history and take hundreds of photographs of the beautiful Corfu villages has been a privilege and a personal triumph. To raise in excess of my £10,000 target has been hard work but is also a testament to the people who have bought the books and their love and passion for our favourite Island and its people. It has also given me the platform to write this book about my life on Corfu which may not have been possible without first serving my amateur writing apprenticeship. With donations, the sale of the eBooks and the sale of the printed books the charity fund will exceed £15,000 and still counting, So, not a bad effort from the people who care and the working class kid from Wolverhampton.

I have learned a lot about the Greek people along the way. The fierce independence and resilience of the Corfiot's. The pride and passion of the village families and their loyalty to one another. The friendliness shown to me by the local Papas. The laughs I have had with the older members of the community, the histories of their villages and their ability to converse with me with every English word they knew. The respect shown by the children of friends who we have seen grow up and have become friends too. The old friends we have come to love as we have all grown older together. The spring catch ups after a cold and wet winter. The great times we have together in the summertime and the tearful goodbyes on the last visit of the season. All these memories and more are what make up the complex tapestry of Corfu and its people. The simple way of life and the genuine generosity all adds to the make up of what it is to be a Phaceaciean. An Island and it's people who have been ruled by many but have never been conquered. A poor strategic outpost which was once an Island of villages inland and fishing villages on the coast. A place that embraced early tourism, became over popularised and then looked forward to a new Corfu with modern ideas. A place where new ideas are welcome but not to the detriment of the local traditions. This is Corfu.

I hope you have enjoyed this book as much as I have writing it. There maybe more stories to come in the future so watch this space as they say and enjoy Corfu.

With the constant promotion of the books and a monthly Corfu charity Blog, people on the Facebook groups were now becoming more aware of the different charities on Corfu and either wanted to help or become more active. There had always been good work being carried out on the Island but now

more and more people knew about it.
Martin and Wendy Brindley set up the
"Friends of Corfu" group and do great
work raising money to buy essentials
for the hospital and the old people's
home. They have a great team based
around the Island and I have a lot of
respect for the work they do on the
ground.

Now that many of you have now
bought the Corfu villages printed book I
am sure you are looking forward to
your next holiday when you can visit
some of the beautiful villages you have
read about. You have probably built up
images of the favourite ones you wish
to visit and having personally visited
over 100 villages I will give you a few
tips on how to get the best from your
experiences. The beauty really is in the

eye of the beholder as you will find out. In the book I have tried to be impartial and treat every village with the same respect as they are all unique and different in their own way. Only by visiting the villages and spending time there will you get the true feel and character of each one. Don't rush around and try to visit as many as you can in one day. Take your time and walk around, look for the Church, the kafeneion, a taverna, the village centre and any sites that are unique to that village.

A morning visit will be the coolest part of the day and you will see the locals as they begin their daily chores, leave for work, head for the kafeneion or the nearest bakery.

An afternoon visit will be the quietest time of the day as the locals will have a siesta and the smaller villages will be deserted. This is a good time to go if you want to take photographs as the light from the sun is at its brightest. It is also the hottest time of day and the most likely time that any shops will be closed so always take a big bottle of water with you and even a picnic lunch just in case.

A visit in the evening sees the village awake and as the sun goes down there are some breath taking sunsets to see. The kafeneion or taverna will open and village comes alive with the sound of Greek music and banter.

There is no bad time to visit a Corfu village, it is entirely up to you and what kind of experience you want to get out of it. We are all different and armed with a little knowledge I am sure you will enjoy them all and find your favourite ones where you will return.

I hope you have enjoyed this book as much as I have writing it. There maybe more stories to come in the future so watch this space as they say and enjoy Corfu.

Kind regards, Steve. x

Printed in Great Britain
by Amazon

46059424R00255